W9-CHX-654

People in the NEWS

The Dalai Lama

by Charles and Linda George

LUCENT BOOKS

A part of Gale, Cengage Learning

GALE
CENGAGE Learning

Detroit • New York • San Francisco • New Haven, Conn • Waterville, Maine • London

GALE
CENGAGE Learning™

LIBRARY OF CONGRESS CATALOGING-IN-PUBLICATION DATA

George, Charles, 1949–
  The Dalai Lama / by Charles and Linda George.
    p. cm. -- (People in the news)
  Includes bibliographical references and index.
  ISBN 978-1-4205-0232-9 (hardcover)
  1. Bstan-'dzin-rgya-mtsho, Dalai Lama XIV, 1935--Juvenile literature.
  2. Dalai lamas--Biography--Juvenile literature. I. George, Linda. II. Title.
  BQ7935.B777G525 2010
  294.3'923092--dc22
  [B]
                                                              2009036534

Lucent Books
27500 Drake Rd.
Farmington Hills, MI 48331

ISBN-13: 978-1-4205-0232-9
ISBN-10: 1-4205-0232-8

Printed in the United States of America
1 2 3 4 5 6 7 13 12 11 10 09

Printed by Bang Printing, Brainerd, MN, 1st Ptg., 12/2009

Contents

F ame and celebrity are alluring. People are drawn to those who walk in fame's spotlight, whether they are known for great accomplishments or for notorious deeds. The lives of the famous pique public interest and attract attention, perhaps because their experiences seem in some ways so different from, yet in other ways so similar to, our own.

Newspapers, magazines, and television regularly capitalize on this fascination with celebrity by running profiles of famous people. For example, television programs such as *Entertainment Tonight* devote all of their programming to stories about entertainment and entertainers. Magazines such as *People* fill their pages with stories of the private lives of famous people. Even newspapers, newsmagazines, and television news frequently delve into the lives of well-known personalities. Despite the number of articles and programs, few provide more than a superficial glimpse at their subjects.

Lucent's People in the News series offers young readers a deeper look into the lives of today's newsmakers, the influences that have shaped them, and the impact they have had in their fields of endeavor and on other people's lives. The subjects of the series hail from many disciplines and walks of life. They include authors, musicians, athletes, political leaders, entertainers, entrepreneurs, and others who have made a mark on modern life and who, in many cases, will continue to do so for years to come.

These biographies are more than factual chronicles. Each book emphasizes the contributions, accomplishments, or deeds that have brought fame or notoriety to the individual and shows how that person has influenced modern life. Authors portray their subjects in a realistic, unsentimental light. For example, Bill Gates—the cofounder and chief executive officer of the software giant Microsoft—has been instrumental in making personal computers the most vital tool of the modern age. Few dispute his business savvy, his perseverance, or his technical expertise, yet critics say he is ruthless in his dealings with competitors and driven more by his desire to maintain Microsoft's dominance in the computer industry than by an interest in furthering technology.

In these books, young readers will encounter inspiring stories about real people who achieved success despite enormous obstacles. Oprah Winfrey—the most powerful, most watched, and wealthiest woman on television today—spent the first six years of her life in the care of her grandparents while her unwed mother sought work and a better life elsewhere. Her adolescence was colored by promiscuity, pregnancy at age fourteen, rape, and sexual abuse.

Each author documents and supports his or her work with an array of primary and secondary source quotations taken from diaries, letters, speeches, and interviews. All quotes are footnoted to show readers exactly how and where biographers derive their information and provide guidance for further research. The quotations enliven the text by giving readers eyewitness views of the life and accomplishments of each person covered in the People in the News series.

In addition, each book in the series includes photographs, annotated bibliographies, timelines, and comprehensive indexes. For both the casual reader and the student researcher, the People in the News series offers insight into the lives of today's newsmakers—people who shape the way we live, work, and play in the modern age.

A Simple Monk

Tenzin Gyatso, a man referred to by his followers and admirers as His Holiness the Fourteenth Dalai Lama, calls himself a simple monk, but he is much more than that. He is a teacher, a religious and spiritual leader, the head of Tibet's government-in-exile, a world traveler, a noted scholar, an author of numerous books, and a sought-after speaker and lecturer. In 2007, during a ceremony in Washington, D.C., to award the Dalai Lama the U.S. Congressional Gold Medal, House Speaker Nancy Pelosi said: "To millions of believers and admirers, he is a source of wisdom and compassion. To young people, he is a positive example of how to make the world a better place."[1]

Tibetans consider him a symbol of religious freedom and their best hope for independence from Communist China. Since 1950 the nation of Tibet has been occupied by armed forces from China and claimed as a part of that nation, which does not tolerate Tibetan Buddhism or any other religion. In 1959 the Dalai Lama and thousands of others fled Tibet to escape religious oppression, and today they still live in exile. Meanwhile, due to a massive influx of Chinese settlers into Tibet, Chinese now outnumber Tibetans in their own country.

Since his escape into India, the Dalai Lama has tirelessly used his position as Tibetans' religious and political leader to educate the rest of the world about conditions in his country and try to influence the Chinese government to agree to grant some measure of autonomy for his people. Another of his goals has been the

Tenzin Gyatso, known as the Dalai Lama, meditates during a visit to Calcutta, India.

preservation of Tibetan culture, which he believes has much to offer the world.

Tibetans call their leader by many names. A few of these are *Kundun, Yishin Norbu, Kyabgon*, and *Gyalwa Rinpoche*. In English, these names mean "Presence," "Savior," "Wish-Fulfilling Gem," and "Precious Victor." Others include "Holy One," "Glorious One," "Mighty of Speech," "Excellent Understanding," "Absolute Wisdom," "Defender of the Faith," and "Ocean."

In the foreword of his book *Freedom in Exile: The Autobiography of the Dalai Lama*, the Dalai Lama defines himself:

> Dalai Lama means different things to different people. To some it means that I am a living Buddha, the earthly manifestation of Avalokiteshvara, Bodhisattva of Compassion. To others it means that I am a "god-king." During the late 1950s it meant that I was a Vice-President of the Steering Committee of the People's Republic of China. Then when I escaped into exile, I was called a counterrevolutionary and a parasite. But none of these are my ideas. To me "Dalai Lama" is a title that signifies the office I hold. I myself am just a human being, and incidentally a Tibetan, who chooses to be a Buddhist monk.[2]

Great Teacher

The title "dalai" means "ocean" in Mongolian. The word "lama" simply means "teacher," much like the Sanskrit term "guru." Together, they can be translated as "ocean teacher" because of the depth of his wisdom and compassion. There are thousands of lamas are in the world. They originally taught and practiced Buddhism only in Tibet and Mongolia, in central Asia, but are now scattered around the world. Each lama must undergo extensive training in Tibetan Buddhist philosophy and ritual before being allowed to teach. In this way, they are similar to Catholic priests, Protestant pastors, Jewish rabbis, and Muslim imams, who must train in their respective faiths until deemed qualified to teach and preach. One major difference, though, separates Buddhist lamas from their counterparts in most other world religions. By Buddhist reckoning, most lamas are hundreds of years old.

Because Buddhists believe in reincarnation—that when a person dies, his or her soul is reborn into another body—they believe great teachers possess souls that have returned, lifetime after lifetime, to lead them. The Dalai Lama is such a teacher. In fact, Tibetans believe that all fourteen dalai lamas, stretching back to the 1300s, have possessed the same soul. Because of this belief they revere the Dalai Lama, considering him a god-king.

Although many non-Buddhists do not believe in reincarnation—and, therefore, do not share the belief in his many lifetimes—millions of people around the world still have enormous respect for the Dalai Lama. His quiet optimism, positive outlook, quick intelligence, radiant good humor, and apparent sense of inner peace, as well as his obvious concern for all humanity, have inspired people of all faiths. For many, it is his exotic appearance—dressed invariably in robes the color of saffron and gold, yet wearing modern eyeglasses and brown Oxford shoes—that intrigues them. For others, it is his quiet, unassuming demeanor, his ever-present smile, and his quick and genuine laugh.

Not everyone shares such a high opinion of this man, however. He has been called a counterrevolutionary and a parasite by Chinese officials. Some see his efforts to preserve Tibetan culture as standing in the way of progress—hanging on to their feudal past. Some believe he stirs up trouble wherever he goes or that he does what he does for his own fame or for monetary gain. Some of his own countrymen disagree with his tactics. Regardless of the debate, people around the world are intrigued by the Dalai Lama and interested to hear what he has to say, in spite of his humble beginnings in one of the most remote regions on Earth.

Chapter 1

Rising from Obscurity

Tenzin Gyatso, the fourteenth dalai lama of Tibet, is a familiar public figure. He speaks to thousands of people each year and has written dozens of best-selling books on his homeland, his life, his religious beliefs, the world's climate, and world affairs. He has been granted honorary degrees from numerous universities, and his face is widely recognized. Yet, this "simple monk" began life in obscurity as Lhamo Thondup, the eighth child born to poor farmers in a tiny village in a remote corner of Tibet.

Taktser, Tibet

In the northeastern corner of historical Tibet lies the province of Amdo, and near the far northeastern edge of that province, only a few miles from the Chinese border, lies the village of Taktser, meaning "Roaring Tiger" in Tibetan. At the time of the fourteenth dalai lama's birth in 1935 (referred to as Wood Hog Year in the Tibetan calendar), Amdo was controlled by a Muslim warlord who had allied himself with China, so some sources list the Dalai Lama's birthplace as Qinghai Province in China rather than Amdo Province in Tibet. Tibetans, however, have always considered Amdo part of their homeland and insist the Dalai Lama is Tibetan. He, of course, agrees.

According to the Dalai Lama, "[Taktser] was a small and poor settlement which stood on a hill overlooking a broad valley. Its pastures had not been settled or farmed for long, only grazed by

The Dalai Lama sits under an elaborately carved gold statue of Buddha. Many believe the Dalai Lama is a living Buddha and the Tibetan god-king.

nomads. The reason for this was the unpredictability of the weather in that area. During my early childhood, my family was one of twenty or so making a precarious living from the land there."[3] His parents, Choekyong and Diki Tsering, farmed barley, buckwheat, and potatoes in the rocky soil. They also raised horses, sheep, goats, a few chickens, and several *dzomos*, which are a cross between a yak and a cow. The barley they raised, when roasted and ground into fine flour, became *tsampa*, a staple of the Tibetan diet. The Dalai Lama still eats *tsampa* every day for breakfast, mixing it with milk, tea, or yogurt.

The Dalai Lama's family lived in a typical house, constructed of stone and mud, painted white, with a tiled roof. In front of the house was a courtyard. A flagpole held banners of multicolored pieces of cloth, stamped with Tibetan Buddhist prayers. The only unique feature of the home was its system of gutters—gouged-out segments of juniper branches—which later played a role in the identification of the Dalai Lama.

In his autobiography *Freedom in Exile*, the Dalai Lama describes his family's house:

> Inside were six rooms; a kitchen, where we spent most of our time when indoors; a prayer-room with a small altar, where we would gather to make offerings at the beginning of the day; my parents' room; a spare room for any guest we might have; a storeroom for our provisions; and finally a byre [a cowshed] for the cattle. There was no bedroom for us children. As a baby, I slept with my mother; then, later, in the kitchen, by the stove.[4]

Life on the arid, wind-swept Tibetan plateau was difficult. Not all children survived. The Dalai Lama's mother gave birth to sixteen children. Seven lived. The Dalai Lama was the eighth to be born, the fifth to survive. Weather also made it a risky place to raise a family. Although the area around Taktser supports agriculture, it receives little rainfall. Often, that precipitation falls as hail. Therefore, crops are sometimes destroyed by drought or hail, causing famine. According to the Dalai Lama's mother, their family survived, sometimes for years, on lentils, rice, and peas provided by the monks from nearby Kumbum monastery.

The Birth of Lhamo Thondup

In the 1930s Tibet had no paved roads, so travel was on foot or on horseback. Currency was uncommon in the remote region, so most commerce involved barter—trading goods for other goods or services. The nearest town, Siling, was three hours away by horse, and the Dalai Lama's father sometimes rode there to exchange what he had grown for supplies such as tea, sugar, cotton cloth, tools, or perhaps a horse.

The three years before Lhamo Thondup's birth were particularly difficult for the family. During that time they received no rain—only hail. Their crops were repeatedly destroyed. Despite the father's knowledge of horses, all their horses went mad, rolling in their drinking water and not eating. Their necks became stiff, they went lame, and all thirteen eventually died. The father felt disgraced because they were his responsibility, but it was never determined what ailment they had contracted, if any. Two months before Lhamo Thondup's birth, his father also became very ill and was bedridden. When he stood, he became dizzy and fainted. Each time he passed out, he saw visions of his dead parents. He could not sleep at night,

Historical Tibet

Historical Tibet no longer exists on maps. Since its invasion in 1949 by China, it has been absorbed into various Chinese provinces. When China refers to Tibet, it means the Tibet Autonomous Region (TAR), an administrative district it created in 1965, which contains less than half the land area of historical Tibet. Historical Tibet—what Tibetans today still refer to as Tibet—originally covered 965,000 square miles (2.5 million sq km)—the size of western Europe or the United States west of the Mississippi River. And yet, despite this region's geographic importance to Asia, little was known about it until relatively recently, largely because of its remoteness and inaccessibility.

kept his wife awake, and made it difficult for her to work during the day.

One month before the child's birth, Diki Tsering had a recurring dream. She saw a brilliant blue dragon and two green snow lions flying through the air. In her memoir, *Dalai Lama, My Son*, she writes,

> They smiled at me and greeted me in the traditional Tibetan style: two hands, raised to the forehead. Later I was told that the dragon was His Holiness [the thirteenth dalai lama], and the two snow lions were the Nechung Oracle (the state fortune-teller of Tibet), showing His Holiness the path to rebirth. After my dream I knew that my child would be some high lama, but never in my wildest dreams did I think that he would be the Dalai Lama.[5]

On July 6, 1935, the morning of Lhamo's birth, his father got out of bed before sunrise, completely well. When he learned his wife had given birth to a son, he told her they should make him a monk. After the birth, the rains came and no more deaths or other odd incidents occurred.

Childhood Memories

As a small child, before his identification by Tibetan lamas, Lhamo never showed any fear of strangers and insisted on sitting at the head of the table. His mother later described her child's uniqueness:

> Lhamo Thondup was different from my other children right from the start. He was a somber child who liked to stay indoors by himself. He was always packing his clothes and his little belongings. When I asked what he was doing, he would reply that he was packing to go to Lhasa [Tibet's capital] and would take all of us with him. When we went to visit friends or relatives, he never drank tea from any cup but mine. He never let anyone except me touch his blankets and he never placed them anywhere but next to mine. If he came across a quarrelsome person, he would pick up a stick and try to beat him. If ever one of our guests lit up a cigarette, he would flare into a rage. Our friends

told us for some unaccountable reason they were afraid of him, tender in years as he was. This was all when he was over a year old and could hardly talk. One day he told us that he had come from heaven.[6]

The Dalai Lama's memories of his parents remain clear. His father, who died in 1947, was a somewhat stern man of medium height, with a bushy mustache and a quick temper. His mother, who died in 1981, was highly regarded. He describes her as "undoubtedly one of the kindest people I have ever known. She was truly wonderful and was loved, I am quite certain, by all who knew her."[7]

For almost three years Lhamo Thondup and his family lived common, everyday lives. He remembers that he loved going into the chicken coop with his mother to collect eggs. When she finished,

Diki Tsering (left), the mother of the Dalai Lama, recognized that Lhamo Thondup was unique even as a small child.

his mother went back to the house, but he stayed, sitting in one of the nests, making clucking noises. He remembers the first time he saw a camel, how huge and frightening it seemed to him. He also remembers seeing a group of children fighting and running to help those being hurt.

Nothing unusual happened during those years. Despite the dreams, expectations, and auspicious events surrounding their son's birth, his parents never imagined their son could be the reincarnation of the most powerful and respected man in Tibet—the thirteenth dalai lama.

The Great Thirteenth

Buddhists believe the essence of each individual—the "higher self" or "soul"—is reborn into a new body once the former body dies. They believe this process continues for generations until the individual reaches enlightenment—a full awakening to the true meaning of life. At that time the individual attains nirvana—ultimate, heavenly peace—and does not have to return to physical life. Since lamas dedicate themselves to spiritual pursuits, they are considered by many to possess "old" souls. Each dalai lama is believed to be the same soul that inhabited the very first dalai lama. Many feel he also is a manifestation of Avalokiteshvara, the bodhisattva of compassion. A bodhisattva is someone who continues to incarnate to help others achieve nirvana.

The thirteenth dalai lama, Thupten Gyatso, was unlike his predecessors. He looked beyond the isolation of Tibet and realized the importance of international affairs. He was the first dalai lama to travel outside Tibet—to Mongolia, China, and India. He modernized Tibet, established a secular educational system, an armory, a defensive force, a postal service, a national flag, and a more sophisticated foreign ministry.

The Great Thirteenth, as he was called, claimed to have visions of the future. In the 1930s he foresaw terrible threats for Tibet twenty years hence. He predicted a time when "monks and monasteries will be destroyed . . . [and] all beings will be sunk in great hardship and overwhelming fear."[8] In 1932 the Great Thirteenth made a drastic choice. He decided to die so his reincarnated self would be old enough to be of some help when those threats occurred. Some lamas have claimed to have such control over their breathing that they can literally "will themselves" to die.

On December 17, 1933, after weeks of sitting in silent meditation, Thupten Gyatso died. He was fifty-seven. His corpse was preserved in the traditional manner for high lamas. It was cooked in yak butter and salt, his face painted with gold, and he was seated upright, facing south, in a shrine in the Potala Palace, the seat of Tibet's government and the Dalai Lama's winter home. According to Tibetan Buddhist belief, his soul went to dwell for forty-nine days in Lake Lhamo Lahtso in southern Tibet before moving to its new incarnation.

The Dalai Lama Lineage

Tibetan Buddhists believe all beings are reincarnated but that certain individuals, called *tulku*s, or incarnations, choose to return again and again to teach others how to achieve nirvana. Highest of these is the Dalai Lama. Thirteen dalai lamas, each one a *tulku*, had reigned in Tibet by the time of Lhamo Thondup's birth in 1935. The first, Gendun Drup, was named Dalai Lama in 1391. When he died in 1474, Tibet's high lamas searched for a child who had been born possessing the soul of Gendun Drup. The reincarnated soul of Gendun Drup was found in a child named Gendun Gyatso, born in 1475. Following Gendun Gyatso's death in 1541, lamas found Sonam Gyatso (1543–1588). Then followed Yonten Gyatso (1589–1616), Lobsang Gyatso (1617–1682), Tsangyang Gyatso (1683–1706), Kelzang Gyatso (1708–1757), Jamphel Gyatso (1758–1804), Lungtok Gyatso (1806–1815), Tsultrim Gyatso (1816–1837), Khendrup Gyatso (1838–1856), Trinley Gyatso (1857–1875), and finally Thupten Gyatso, who was born in 1876. "Gyatso" is the Tibetan word for "ocean," symbolizing the depth and breadth of their wisdom.

Finding and Testing the Fourteenth Dalai Lama

After Thupten Gyatso's death, lamas began searching for the fourteenth dalai lama as soon as signs appeared. Traditionally, visions and omens lead lamas to the next incarnation. The first sign after Thupten Gyatso's death came from the deceased dalai lama himself. Despite his having been placed facing south, his head mysteriously turned northeast. The lamas, therefore, searched northeast for his successor.

The next sign appeared in the form of a vision that came to one of the senior lamas, Reting Rinpoché. Rinpoché is a title given to

Lamas found the young successor to the Dalai Lama lineage thanks to a sign from the deceased Thupten Gyatso as well as spiritual visions.

"Roof of the World"

Mount Everest, the world's tallest mountain peak, towers above Tibet's southern border.

When people think of Tibet, most picture high, snow-capped mountains. Tibet contains some of the tallest mountains in the world, including the tallest—Mount Everest (*Chomo Langma* to Tibetans), at 29,028 feet (8,848m). The Himalayas form almost the entire southern border of Tibet. Another lesser-known feature of this remote land is the Tibetan Plateau, a high, windswept region that makes up the majority of Tibet's land area. Because of the Himalayas and the Tibetan Plateau, Tibet's average elevation—16,000 feet (4,880m)—is higher than all but the tallest peaks in the North American Rockies.

The vast Tibetan Plateau also serves as origin for many of the mightiest rivers in Asia. The Yellow and Yangtze rivers flow eastward off the Tibetan Plateau and through China to the Yellow Sea and the East China Sea, respectively. The Indus, Ganges, and Brahmaputra rivers flow southward from Tibet—through India, Pakistan, and Bangladesh—before emptying into the Arabian Sea and the Bay of Bengal. Finally, the Salween and Mekong rivers flow through Southeast Asia and into the Indian Ocean and the South China Sea, respectively. Together, the water from these seven rivers that originate in Tibet sustains the lives of 40 percent of Earth's population.

spiritual masters. It means "Precious One." Reting Rinpoché visited the sacred lake of Lhamo Lahtso and saw the Tibetan letters *Ah, Ka,* and *Ma* floating in the lake. He was sure *Ah* referred to Amdo Province in northeastern Tibet. He also saw a vision of a three-story monastery with a turquoise and gold roof and a small house with strangely shaped rain gutters. A party of monks was sent to Amdo. After four years of searching, they arrived at Kumbum monastery, which stood three stories tall and had a turquoise and gold roof. This, they were sure, represented *Ka* from the lake vision. Nearby, they located a house with gutters made from gnarled juniper branches. Inside, they found a farming family with a toddler—Lhamo Thondup.

The group's leader, Khetsang Rinpoché, a high-ranking monk from the Sera monastery near Lhasa, was disguised as a peasant, and yet two-year-old Lhamo still ran to greet him, calling, "Sera lama, Sera lama!" The monks said nothing. They stayed the night, thanked the family for their hospitality, and left the following morning. They returned three weeks later and again stayed with the family, observing the child. They left without informing the family of the purpose of either visit.

On their third visit, two weeks later, they brought a bowl, a ceremonial drum, a rosary, and some clothing that had belonged to Thupten Gyatso, along with similar items that had not. They showed them to Lhamo to see which he preferred. Each time, the child quickly selected the former dalai lama's possessions, saying, "It's mine. It's mine." The Dalai Lama's mother vividly recalls one such test: "Khetsang Rinpoché was carrying two staffs as he entered our veranda, where Lhamo . . . was playing. Rinpoché put both staffs in a corner. Our son went to the staffs, laid one aside and picked up the other. He struck Rinpoché lightly on the back with it, said that staff was his and why had Khetsang Rinpoché taken it."[9]

Only then did the monks reveal their true purpose—to locate the reincarnation of their former leader. They had tested several possible candidates in the region but were convinced *this* was the child they sought. After visiting with Lhamo for three more hours in private, the monks told Lhamo's mother that her son had spoken to them, without difficulty, in their own Lhasa dialect. He had never heard that dialect spoken before.

The Long Wait at Kumbum

It was not uncommon in those days for very young boys—some as young as two—to be admitted to Tibetan monasteries to be trained as Buddhist monks. The Dalai Lama remembers those first months at Kumbum as a particularly unhappy time of his life because his parents did not remain there with him. But several factors made Lhamo's stay at Kumbum a bit easier to bear.

One brother, Lobsang Samten, had earlier been identified as a *tulku*, the reincarnation of a high lama, and was already in training at the monastery. Although Lobsang was only three years older, he cared for Lhamo, and they became inseparable. Another thing that helped the toddler through this time of separation was the temperament of the teacher assigned to him for preliminary training. The Dalai Lama remembers him as a very kind, older monk who comforted him as well as taught him, sometimes wrapping him in his gown and giving him special treats. Finally, when it was made clear to Lhamo that he would be reunited with his parents as soon as preparations were made for his journey to Lhasa, he was better able to endure his loneliness.

They were convinced. After informing the family, they dispatched a messenger to Lhasa to inform the interim ruler—the regent—that the new dalai lama had been found. Aware it would take several weeks to receive a response, it was decided that Lhamo should go to Kumbum monastery to be installed and to begin his training. The Dalai Lama recalls, "I was installed in a ceremony that took place at dawn. I remember this fact particularly as I was surprised to be woken and dressed before the sun had risen. I also remember being seated on a throne."[10] Thus began the journey that has taken the Dalai Lama far beyond Tibet.

Chapter 2

Life in Lhasa

Shortly after being identified as the fourteenth dalai lama, young Lhamo Thondup was taken by his parents to Kumbum monastery to begin preliminary religious training and to wait while preparations were made for his journey to Lhasa. Eighteen months later, the new Dalai Lama's procession began its three-month trek to the nation's capital. Once there, he would be enthroned as the spiritual leader of the Tibetan people, and after years of further training, their political leader as well. True to the thirteenth dalai lama's predictions, the new Dalai Lama would eventually be forced to lead his nation against an ominous threat.

Journey to Lhasa

In July 1939, a week after Lhamo's fourth birthday, his formal procession departed Kumbum for Lhasa. The procession consisted of the young Dalai Lama, his parents, his brother Lobsang Samten, the search party, a few government officials, a number of religious pilgrims, and guides who knew the route well. Most members of the procession walked or rode mules or horses. The newly recognized Dalai Lama, however, rode in style with his brother in a palanquin called a *dreljam*, an enclosed wooden compartment with a couch or cushions, suspended on poles between two mules.

During their long journey, he and his brother acted like young siblings the world over. They argued and scuffled. The Dalai Lama describes their behavior:

We spent a great deal of time squabbling and arguing, as small children do, and often came to blows. This put our conveyance in danger of overbalancing. At that point the driver would stop the animals and summon my mother. When she looked inside, she always found the same thing: Lobsang Samten in tears and me sitting there with a look of triumph on my face.[11]

The new Dalai Lama is carried by an attendant during the journey to Lhasa for the installment ceremony.

When the party neared Lhasa, it was met by senior government officials. After a daylong welcoming ceremony, the Dalai Lama and his brother were taken to Norbulingka Palace, the Dalai Lama's summer residence, west of Lhasa. One memory of his early days there provided further evidence of his identity. When he and his family first arrived in Lhasa, he told his mother that his teeth were in a box in one of the houses at the Norbulingka compound. Monks later found a small wooden box containing a set of dentures. The false teeth had belonged to the thirteenth dalai lama.

The Lion Throne and the Potala Palace

In the winter of 1940, when Lhamo was still four years old, he was taken to the Potala Palace for his formal installation ceremony. The Potala, besides being the Dalai Lama's winter home and center of Tibet's government, also contained one of the largest monasteries in the country. On February 22, 1940, Lhamo Thondup first occupied the Lion Throne—the huge, jewel-encrusted, ornately carved wooden structure that had served Tibet's god-kings for centuries. His enthronement ceremony took place in *Si shi phuntsog*—the Hall of All Good Deeds of the Spiritual and Temporal World—the principal stateroom in the east wing of the palace.

The ceremony installed him as spiritual leader of Tibet. Shortly thereafter, he went to the Jokhang temple in the center of the city for the remainder of his induction. At Jokhang his head was shaved and he was given the maroon robes of a novice (beginner) monk. He also assumed the name Jamphel Ngawang Lobsang Yeshe Tenzin Gyatso.

Immediately after his induction as a novice monk, Tenzin Gyatso began his formal education. He was assigned three tutors, one of whom was Khetsang Rinpoché, leader of the party that identified him in Amdo. His first lessons involved reading. He and his brother studied together. In their classrooms, he recalls, were

two whips, a yellow silk one and a leather one. The former, we were told, was reserved for the Dalai Lama and

The Potala Palace

The Potala Palace dominates Lhasa, overlooking the city from atop a rocky outcrop called Red Hill. The structure is listed as a World Heritage Site by the United Nations. Built during the seventeenth century—during the reign of the fifth dalai lama—the structure covers 5 square miles (13 sq km) and contains one thousand rooms. Until 1959 it served not only as the Dalai Lama's winter residence but also housed Tibet's government offices, the tombs of eight dalai lamas, a monastery serving 175 monks, numerous chapels and religious statues, storerooms filled with the nation's treasures, staterooms for governmental and religious ceremonies, and a school for young monks. With Tibet today under Chinese control and the Dalai Lama living in exile, the Potala has been converted to a museum.

The grandiose Potala Palace in Lhasa covers 5 square miles (13 sq km) and overlooks the city.

the latter was for the Dalai Lama's brother. These instruments of torture terrified us both. It took only a glance from our teacher at one or other of these whips to make me shiver with fear. Happily, the yellow one was never used, although the leather one came off the wall once or twice.[12]

His bedroom in the Potala once belonged to the fifth dalai lama and occupied the seventh floor, high above the city. He remembers it as a cold, dimly lit room, seemingly unoccupied since the seventeenth century:

Everything in it was ancient and decrepit and, behind the drapes that hung across each of the four walls lay deposits of centuries-old dust. At one end of the room stood an altar. On it were set small butter lamps (bowls of rancid *dri* [yak] butter into which a wick was set and lighted) and little dishes of food and water placed in offering to the Buddhas. Every day these would be plundered by mice. I became very fond of these little creatures. They were very beautiful and showed no fear as they helped themselves to their daily rations. At night, as I lay in bed, I would hear these companions of mine running to and fro. Sometimes they came over to my bed. This was the only substantial piece of furniture in my room, other than the altar, and consisted of a large wooden box filled with cushions and surrounded by long, red curtains. The mice would clamber over these too, their urine dripping down as I snuggled under my blankets below.[13]

During those years, he and his brother were not allowed to have playmates their own age, but others in the palaces kept them company. Tenzin Gyatso had three personal attendant monks—Master of the Ritual, Master of the Robes, and Master of the Kitchen. Also, several middle-aged men of little or no education served as sweepers, cleaning the palaces. These men became the boys' playmates. When Lobsang Samten later left to attend private school, Tenzin Gyatso had only his attendants and the sweepers for companionship. His mother and sister visited occasionally, but over the years he had little contact with his family.

A Typical Day of Study

After a few years, Tenzin Gyatso began more extensive lessons. His day began at 6:00 AM with an hour of prayer and meditation, followed by breakfast, then a penmanship class. The Tibetan written language is quite elaborate, requiring a great deal of practice. After penmanship came memorization class, where he learned Buddhist texts he would recite later in the day. At 10:00 he attended governmental meetings to help him prepare for the day he would assume political leadership of Tibet. After these meetings he returned to his quarters, where his junior tutor listened to him recite passages he had learned that morning. At noon a conch shell was blown, indicating playtime.

Like most boys, playtime was Tenzin Gyatso's favorite activity. He was fortunate to have a good collection of toys, many given to him by visiting dignitaries. One favorite was a Meccano erector set, an assortment of reusable metal strips, plates, angle girders, wheels, axles, and gears, with nuts and bolts, used to construct mechanical devices. Other favorites were a train set and some lead soldiers. He later melted down the soldiers and recast them as monks. He liked playing soldier with the sweepers, too, because many had served in the army.

About 1:00 came a light lunch, followed by general education classes, which Tenzin Gyatso disliked. The subjects included logic, Tibetan art and culture, medicine, Buddhist philosophy, and Sanskrit, an ancient written language from India. He also studied poetry, music and drama, astrology, synonyms, and public speaking. Tenzin Gyatso's most difficult and most important subjects were Buddhist philosophy—the precepts and teachings of the Buddha and early Buddhist philosophers—and debate. It is through debating with other monks that a student's intellect is judged. After his general classes, his tutors spent the next hour explaining how to debate the day's topic.

After those classes, usually around 4:00, tea was served. Tibetan tea is traditionally mixed with salt and yak butter instead of milk. After tea, two monks arrived, and he spent the next hour debating questions like "What is the nature of mind?" Finally, around 5:30 the day's lessons were complete. As soon as the tutor left, Tenzin

Gyatso rushed to the roof for another favorite activity—looking through his telescope.

Around 7:00, he came downstairs to have his evening meal, usually with monks from the Potala's Namgyal monastery. After eating, he was supposed to go into the courtyard, seven floors below his quarters, to walk, recite scripture, and pray. He admits, "When I was young and still carefree, I hardly ever did so. Instead, I would spend the time either thinking up stories or anticipating the ones that would be told me before going to bed. Very

A boy builds a working drawbridge with an erector set. The erector set was one of the Dalai Lama's favorite toys during his time studying at the Potala Palace.

often, these were of a supernatural nature, so it would be a very scared Dalai Lama who crept into his dark, vermin-infested bedroom at nine o'clock."[14]

Glimpses of the Outside World

The Dalai Lama admits that he did not always take his studies seriously when he was a young monk. Once, when his tutors became concerned he was not making enough progress, they staged exams to show him what little he had learned. They secretly coached one of the uneducated sweepers and tested him alongside the young monk. Tenzin Gyatso was humiliated when the sweeper defeated him, and for a time he studied harder but soon fell back into his lazier ways. In his autobiography he says he did not value formal education until he was older and now regrets not having focused more on his studies in those early days.

In 1944 Tenzin Gyatso's education broadened beyond his tutors' lessons when he located two hand-cranked movie projectors and several rolls of film in a Potala storeroom. He finally located an old Chinese monk who knew how to repair the projectors and who taught him how to use them. He watched each film over and over. One newsreel covered the 1911 coronation of England's king George V. Another taught him about the hazards of gold mining. A third contained footage with special cinematic effects showing female dancers emerging from huge eggs.

Some years later, the British royal family sent the Dalai Lama an electric projector with its own generator. These items instilled in the young monk a keen interest in the inner workings of mechanical objects, and he taught himself a great deal by tinkering with them. He particularly enjoyed examining a gold Rolex watch, sent to him as a gift by American president Franklin D. Roosevelt, and a motion-picture camera.

The storerooms of the Potala became gold mines for the inquisitive child. In addition to the nation's gold and silver treasures and its priceless religious artifacts, he found old swords, flintlock guns, suits of armor, and illustrated books in English about World War I. Young Tenzin Gyatso pored over these volumes, learning all he could about the outside world. He also found

A World at War

By 1944, when Tenzin Gyatso was nine years old, the outside world was at war. World War II had begun in 1939, when Nazi Germany invaded Poland. By 1944 the war was at its height, involving most of the industrialized nations of the world. In that year, the D-Day invasion took place in Europe, the largest military operation in the history of the world. In the Pacific, the tide had turned against the Japanese, and the Allied invasion of the Philippines was in progress. In Tibet, however, life went on as usual. While the world's powers battled, Tenzin Gyatso, isolated in Lhasa, was largely ignorant of what was going on outside his nation.

German soldiers march through the streets of Poland in 1939.

old music boxes, which he took apart, and two pairs of European shoes, which he wore. Nothing he found, though, helped him understand the outside world more than the lessons he received from a most unexpected new tutor—an escaped Austrian prisoner of war named Heinrich Harrer.

Heinrich Harrer

In 1946, when Tenzin Gyatso was eleven years old, an Austrian adventurer and mountaineer, Heinrich Harrer, arrived in Lhasa. He had escaped a British prisoner-of-war camp in India in 1944 and had fled into Tibet with one companion. Together, they made their way across the Himalayas and wandered for two

Austrian adventurer Heinrich Harrer became a tutor, friend, and confidant to the Dalai Lama.

years before arriving in Lhasa. By that time, Harrer had learned to speak Tibetan.

In his autobiography *Seven Years in Tibet*, Harrer records seeing the young Dalai Lama during a New Year Festival at the Potala:

> When we came into the hall of audience, we craned our necks to get a sight of the Living Buddha [the Dalai Lama] over a forest of heads. And he, too, momentarily forgetful of his dignity, looked up eagerly to get a glimpse of the two strangers of whom he had heard so much. In the posture of the Buddha, leaning slightly forward, the Dalai Lama was sitting on a throne covered with costly brocade. For hours he had to sit and watch the faithful filing by and bless them as they passed. . . . When we found ourselves standing with bowed heads before the Presence, I could not resist the temptation to look up. An eager, boyish smile lit up the charming face of the Dalai Lama, and his hand raised in blessing was laid for an instant on my head. . . . None of the visitors came empty-handed. . . . More impressive than the gifts [they brought] is the expression of intense devotion on the faces of all these people. For many it is the greatest moment of their lives.[15]

Tenzin Gyatso, through an intermediary, asked Harrer to film activities outside the palace that he could not attend. Because of his status as god-king, he could not leave the palace without a procession. Neither was he supposed to speak directly to individuals other than his tutors, servants, or family members. Harrer filmed several events, and as the Dalai Lama's collection of films increased, he asked Harrer to build a theater at Norbulingka.

After its completion in 1949, Tenzin Gyatso shocked everyone by disregarding established protocol and inviting Harrer to visit him, in person, at the theater. To Harrer's amazement, the young Dalai Lama greeted him at the door, asked his help with the projector, watched several films with him, and then, while seated casually on the carpet of the theater, bombarded him with dozens of questions about the outside world. Harrer remembers their first face-to-face meeting:

When we were alone we cleared away the films and put the yellow covers on the machines. Then we sat down on a magnificent carpet in the theater with the sun streaming through the open windows. . . . At the start I had wished to decline his invitation to sit down, knowing that even ministers were not supposed to sit in his presence, but he just took me by the sleeve and pulled me down, which put an end to my misgivings. He told me that he had long been planning this meeting, as he had not been able to think of any other way of becoming acquainted with the outside world. He expected the regent to raise objections, but he was determined to have his own way. . . . He was resolved to extend his knowledge beyond purely religious subjects, and it seemed to him that I was the only person who could help him to do so.[16]

Once their relationship was established, Harrer became one of Tenzin Gyatso's tutors, seeing him informally once a week. During the next year and a half, the Austrian helped him learn English, informed him about Europe and the recent world war, and helped him repair some of the mechanical objects he possessed, including the generator and three automobiles that had belonged to his predecessor. At one point, Tenzin Gyatso became so curious about the cars that he sneaked out to one of them and drove it around the grounds of the Norbulingka. Not surprisingly, he ran the car into a tree.

Harrer remained in Tibet until the Chinese invasion in 1950. The Dalai Lama considered him a close friend and stayed in touch with Harrer until he died in Austria in 2006 at the age of ninety-three.

Tough Decisions

In August 1950, when Tenzin Gyatso was fifteen years old, Tibet suffered a major earthquake. Like most Tibetans, he considered this more than a natural phenomenon. He believed it was an evil omen. Two days later, word arrived that Chinese troops had crossed into far northeastern Tibet. China had recently had a revolution and was controlled by the Communist Party and its leader,

Mao Ze-dong, whose aim was the liberation of the people of Tibet from what it considered a repressive feudal government.

At the time of this first attack, the teenage Dalai Lama had not
been declared the political leader of Tibet, so the regent handled
the situation, activating Tibet's relatively small army. However,
two months later, word came that the Chinese military, the People's Liberation Army, had invaded Tibet with eighty thousand
troops. Tibet's leaders realized their eighty-five-hundred-man
army would be no match for the invaders. With winter approach-

In this rare image from 1950, Communist Chinese troops construct a bridge over a swift Tibetan river while a vehicle and supplies are transported across the water on rubber rafts.

ing, the Tibetan people demanded that Tenzin Gyatso be declared an adult, old enough to take charge of the government. He did not believe he was ready, but no one consulted him. Instead, they asked the Nechung Oracle.

In a trance and staggering under the burden of his heavy ceremonial headdress, the oracle "came over to where [the Dalai Lama] sat and laid a *kata*, a white silk offering scarf, on [his] lap with the words 'Thu-la bap,' 'His time has come.' Dorje Drakden [the protector divinity of Tibet, who Tibetan Buddhists believe communicates through the oracle] had spoken."[17] On November 17, 1950, in a ceremony in the Potala Palace, Tenzin Gyatso, the fourteenth Dalai Lama, was officially named political leader of Tibet. Once the ceremony ended, the young monk became the undisputed leader of six million Tibetans, facing full-scale war. The choices before him were daunting.

Chapter 3

Into Exile

A s serious as Tibet's situation was, the young Dalai Lama could pursue only one of three possible courses of action —fight, flee, or negotiate. He could muster his nation's meager, poorly equipped, poorly trained army and send them to face a far superior military force, knowing he would almost certainly be condemning his troops to death and his nation to eventual defeat. He could flee the country, but that would leave his people leaderless and still at the mercy of invaders. Or, he could remain in Tibet and try to negotiate an agreement with China to protect his people and their culture. In order to make the right decision, he had to know more about China.

The Dalai Lama's Difficult Choice

The Dalai Lama admits he knew little about China when he became Tibet's leader, and even less about Chinese Communists. He learned a shocking lesson when, two weeks before the ceremony that was to place him at the head of Tibet's government, his eldest brother, Taktser Rinpoché, arrived in Lhasa from their home province of Amdo. As abbot of Kumbum monastery, Taktser had dealt with Chinese Communists already occupying the province. Taktser's physical appearance alarmed Tenzin Gyatso, who almost did not recognize his brother. He appeared anxious and under tremendous stress, and the news he brought was even more disturbing.

The Dalai Lama was offically named poltical leader of Tibet when he was just fifteen years old.

To the Dalai Lama's dismay, his brother told him he had been sent by Chinese officials to convince his brother to accept Chinese rule of Tibet. Failing that, the officials had instructed Taktser Rinpoché to kill his younger brother. This command indicated how poorly Chinese Communists understood Tibetan Buddhist beliefs. To a Buddhist, all life is sacred, and the idea of one monk killing another—especially his brother—was ludicrous. Taktser Rinpoché decided the only way he could warn his brother was to pretend to obey the orders and then reveal the Communists' treachery when he got to Lhasa. He advised his brother to flee the country, contact the American government for assistance, and send Tibet's army to fight the Chinese.

Faced with this new information, but reluctant to commit the army, the new Tibetan leader consulted the members of the *Kashag*, his inner cabinet of advisers. They decided to send emissaries to Great Britain, the United States, and Nepal to ask for assistance. Another was sent to China to try to negotiate a withdrawal of Chinese troops from eastern Tibet.

A Shocking Announcement

While awaiting replies, the Dalai Lama took the Tibetan seals of state—the metal emblems of Tibet's government, used to imprint official documents—and moved to Dromo, a town in southern Tibet, with key members of his government. This would allow him to quickly escape to India and set up a government in exile should China invade central Tibet. Weeks later, three of the Tibetan envoys returned and reported they had been turned away. No foreign government was willing to help. Only the envoy to China had been received.

About the same time, the Dalai Lama received distressing news from the governor of Chamdo in southeastern Tibet. His province was already under Chinese control, and Chinese officials had threatened to march on Lhasa unless some political settlement was reached. The governor volunteered to go to Peking (now Beijing), China, to negotiate. The Dalai Lama reluctantly agreed and sent two officials from Dromo with him.

Several weeks later, the Dalai Lama was shocked to hear on Radio Beijing that an agreement had been signed between China and Tibet. The representatives had not been authorized to sign such an agreement. However, Chinese radio announced a "Seventeen-Point Agreement for the Peaceful Liberation of Tibet." The first clause of this so-called agreement stated: "The Tibetan people shall unite and drive out imperialist aggressive forces from Tibet. The Tibetan people shall return to the big family of the Motherland—the People's Republic of China."[18] The Dalai Lama knew that the government of Tibet had signed no such document and that Tibet had never been part of China. He suspected that the Tibetan representatives were coerced into signing and that the Chinese used counterfeit state seals to make it appear official.

Many of the Dalai Lama's advisers urged him to flee to India at once. Taktser Rinpoché and Heinrich Harrer, both by this time already in India, sent letters urging him to leave Tibet. Others, however, wanted him to return to Lhasa because the Tibetan people were frightened and needed his leadership. Following a meeting in Dromo with the new Chinese governor-general of Tibet, General Chiang Chin-wu, the Dalai Lama returned to Lhasa.

Six weeks after arriving in Lhasa, after a nine-month absence, the Dalai Lama's worst fears materialized. On October 26, 1951, three thousand Chinese troops entered the city. Eventually, more than twenty thousand troops of the People's Liberation Army were stationed in Lhasa. An uneasy truce remained between the occupying Chinese forces and what Beijing called the "local government" of Tibet. Over the next few years, Chinese officials tightened their grip on the Tibetan people by forcing resignations from government officials they deemed hostile, by bombarding Tibet with Communist propaganda, and by enacting repressive laws.

To Beijing and Back

In 1954 the Dalai Lama was invited to visit China. Many Tibetans feared he would be held there against his will and they would never see him again, but he thought it was a good idea. Not only would he meet and speak directly with Chairman Mao Ze-dong

Political Reforms, Despite Occupation

Between 1951 and 1959 the Dalai Lama, still focusing on his studies, had to walk a virtual political tightrope, trying to avoid a full-scale military takeover of his nation while trying to placate Tibetan resistance fighters. During that time he enacted reforms in Tibet's government, intent on modernizing it. He established an independent judiciary and worked to develop an educational system open to more than just monastic students. He also addressed public audiences, something no previous dalai lama had done. This new openness led to a more personal relationship between him and the common people of Tibet.

but also see something of the outside world. It would be his first voyage outside Tibet. Traveling by jeep, car, mule, train, airplane, and even animal-skin boat, he and an entourage of five hundred made their way to Beijing.

Though much of what he saw in China impressed him and his welcome seemed cordial enough, he still suspected China's motives. The more he learned about Marxism, the philosophy behind Communism, the more he liked it, because it stressed equality and justice for everyone. However, he disagreed with its focus on materialism and with the methods China used to accomplish Marxist goals.

The Dalai Lama met with Chairman Mao a dozen times during his visit to Beijing. Each time, he was impressed with Mao's appearance and his seemingly sincere concern for the people and culture of Tibet. Something the Communist leader whispered to him at the end of their final meeting, in the spring of 1955, however, gave the Dalai Lama serious misgivings about the future of Chinese-Tibetan relations. "He drew closer to me and said, '. . . Religion is poison. Firstly it reduces the population, because

Chairman Mao Ze-dong (middle) meets with the Dalai Lama (right) and Panchen Lama (left) in Beijing, China, during the mid-1950s.

monks and nuns must stay celibate, and secondly it neglects material progress.' At this I felt a violent burning sensation all over my face and I was suddenly very afraid."[19]

The next day, the Dalai Lama departed Beijing to return to Tibet, convinced Communist China had no intention of honoring any agreements about preserving Tibet's cultural heritage but still unsure about what to do. On his way back to Lhasa, his entourage passed through his home village of Taktser. Tibetans there, as in every village he passed, flocked to see him and receive his blessing. In his autobiography, he reports what he saw in their eyes. "When I spoke to Tibetans there, asking about their living conditions, they replied that, 'Thanks to Chairman Mao, to Communism and the People's Republic of China, we are very happy'—but with tears in their eyes."[20]

The Situation Worsens

Over the next couple of years, it became obvious to the Dalai Lama that the Chinese Communists occupying his nation were not going to allow him to effectively lead his people. According to Robert A.F. Thurman, professor of Indo-Tibetan studies at Columbia University, the Dalai Lama, upon his return from China "began to experience the reality of the invasion as the Chinese generals in charge of Tibet broke promise after promise. The Chinese created food shortages, expropriated [seized] lands and goods, began to brainwash common Tibetans, and violently persecuted the majority, who would not agree to their ideas."[21] In addition, reports came to the Dalai Lama that Buddhist monks and nuns were "subject to severe harassment and publicly humiliated. For example, they were forced to join in extermination programmes of insects, rats, birds, and all types of vermin, even though the Chinese authorities knew that taking any form of life is contrary to Buddhist teaching. If they refused, they were beaten."[22]

Several events between 1956 and 1959 eventually helped convince the Dalai Lama of the necessity of leaving Tibet. The first of these, which he initially did not fully understand, occurred in early 1956. Each year during *Losar*, the Tibetan New Year celebration, the Dalai Lama traditionally consults the Nechung Oracle about

Tibet's future. This year the oracle "announced that 'the light of the Wish-Fulfilling Jewel [one of the names by which the Dalai Lama is known to Tibetans] will shine in the West.'"[23] The Dalai Lama interpreted this to mean that he would later travel to India for Buddha Jynati, the upcoming celebration of the twenty-five hundredth anniversary of the Buddha's birth. Only later did he realize that the message had deeper meaning.

In November 1956, after weeks of tense negotiations with Chinese officials in Lhasa, the Dalai Lama was allowed to leave Tibet and travel to India. It was an opportunity to make a pilgrimage

to what Tibetan Buddhists called the "Land of the Holy," the birthplace of the Buddha. It also allowed him to make contact with the Indian government, to explore his options, and to observe the inner workings of India's democracy. In India, the young Dalai Lama was welcomed by throngs of Buddhists from across Asia. According to a *Time* magazine report, "He was surrounded by a whirl of waving yellow prayer flags, burning incense and flower

The Dalai Lama is transported by a decorated donkey while visiting India for the first time in 1956.

petals. Thousands of Buddhist pilgrims prostrated themselves before him, and when they could not touch his gown, they touched the hoofs of his pony."[24]

Indian prime minister Pandit Nehru did not seem to approve of the idea of the Dalai Lama leaving Tibet and fleeing to India. He feared retribution by the Chinese against India. Several of the Dalai Lama's relatives and advisers, though, urged him to remain in India. The Dalai Lama, still hesitant about abandoning his country, again consulted the oracle and then decided to return once more to Lhasa. He departed India with "a heavy heart." His mood further darkened when he approached the Tibetan border and saw, "fluttering amongst the colourful Tibetan prayer-flags . . . at least a dozen blood-red banners proclaiming the People's Republic of China."[25] It was March 1957.

The Road to Exile

From mid-1957 to early 1959, Tibet's fate at the hands of the Chinese became clearer. The Dalai Lama's only alternative was fleeing into exile. In midsummer 1957 open warfare in eastern Tibet between Tibetan rebels and Chinese soldiers brought refugees to Lhasa with horrifying stories of Chinese atrocities. Realizing disaster was looming, the Dalai Lama decided he should rush his final monastic examinations to be better prepared for what was coming. He concentrated on his studies. During the following summer, he traveled to several monasteries to be tested in debates. The final portion of his examination occurred during *Monlam*, the annual Great Prayer Festival held at the Jokhang temple, one of the holiest shrines in Tibet. He passed, receiving his degree along with the title of *geshe* (doctor of Buddhist studies) on March 5, 1959.

Two days later the Dalai Lama received a seemingly innocent invitation from Chinese officials in Lhasa. A new dance troupe had recently arrived from China, and they wanted him to attend. Chinese officials insisted the show be staged at their military headquarters and that no Tibetan soldiers accompany the Dalai Lama to the event. News of these restrictions spread through Lhasa's population, and on the morning of March 10 a huge crowd gath-

Chinese Atrocities in Eastern Tibet

Midsummer of 1957 brought open warfare between rebels in eastern Tibet and the People's Liberation Army. Although refugees flooded into Lhasa from that region with stories of Chinese brutality, few could accept the truth of their tales. Two years later, the Dalai Lama received a copy of an official report by the International Commission of Jurists (ICJ). The ICJ is a nongovernmental organization, headquartered in Geneva, Switzerland, whose aim is to foster understanding of and respect for the rule of law. Their report finally caused him to accept what he had heard, that "crucifixion, vivisection [mutilation], disemboweling and dismemberment of victims was commonplace. So too were beheading, burning, beating to death and burying alive, not to mention dragging people behind galloping horses until they died or hanging them upside down or throwing them bound hand and foot into icy water. And, in order to prevent them shouting out, 'Long live the Dalai Lama', on the way to execution, they tore out their tongues with meat hooks." The ICJ's 1959 report, "The Question of Tibet and the Rule of Law," was based on hundreds of interviews with Tibetan refugees in northern India and, in part, accused Chinese forces of "Wanton killing of Tibetans and other acts capable of leading to the extinction of the Tibetans as a national and religious group, to the extent that it becomes necessary to consider the question of Genocide."

Tenzin Gyatso, the Fourteenth Dalai Lama of Tibet, *Freedom in Exile: The Autobiography of the Dalai Lama*. New York: HarperCollins, 1990, p. 124.

Quoted in Rodney Gilbert, *Genocide in Tibet: A Study of Communist Aggression*. New York: American-Asian Educational Exchange, 1959, p. 35.

ered outside Norbulingka Palace. Fearing the Chinese invitation was a ruse to capture and imprison the Dalai Lama, the people armed themselves with sticks, shovels, and knives and formed a human barrier to protect him and prevent him from attending.

A long line of Tibetans surrenders to troops of China's People's Liberation Army following a failed rebellion at the Potala Palace.

By noon, about thirty thousand people had gathered, surrounding Norbulingka. The Dalai Lama, fearing the mob might take more drastic action and attack the Chinese garrison, announced he would not attend the production. Despite his announcement, the crowd remained, growing in numbers and in spirit. The only thing he could do to defuse the situation was to leave. Without

his presence in the palace, he felt the crowd would disperse, and the people would not be in such imminent danger. His decision was troubling. In his first autobiography, *My Land and My People*, he writes:

> The mental stress of that morning was something I had not experienced before during the brief period of my leadership of the people of Tibet. I felt as if I were standing between two volcanoes, each likely to erupt at any moment. . . . The Lhasan people would be ruthlessly massacred in thousands, and Lhasa and the rest of Tibet would see a fullscale military rule with all its persecution and tyranny.[26]

Eyewitness Report of Chinese Reaction

"As the Dalai Lama and his escort fled by night and hid by day in lamaseries [Buddhist monasteries], villages and Khamba [Tibetan rebels] encampments, the furious Red Chinese boasted that they had put down the three-day revolt in Lhasa that had served to cover the god-king's escape. Point-blank artillery fire drove diehard lamas from the Norbulingka, summer palace on the city's outskirts. Red infantrymen surged into the vast warrens of the Potala winter palace, rounded up defiant monks in narrow passages and dark rooms where flickering butter lamps made Tibet's grotesque gods and demons seem to caper on the walls. The corpses of hundreds of slain Lhasans lay in the streets and parks of the city, from the gutted medical college on Chakpori hill to the barricaded main avenue of Barkhor. Rifle fire and the hammer of machine guns rattled the windows of the Indian consulate general, whose single radio transmitter is the only communication link with the free world. And Red Chinese columns and planes crisscrossed the barren plateaus and narrow valleys of Tibet in search of the missing Dalai Lama."

Time, "The Three Precious Jewels," April 20, 1959. www.time.com/time/magazine/article/0,9171,864579,00.html.

Escape

After a week, with the crowd of armed supporters still surrounding the palace, the Dalai Lama consulted the Nechung oracle. The oracle shouted, "Go! Go! Tonight!" and wrote specific instructions about how to flee the city unnoticed. All that day, March 17, 1959, secret plans were made. In the afternoon, the Dalai Lama's tutors and members of the *Kashag* left the palace, hidden under a tarp in the back of a truck. In the evening, his mother and several other women left secretly. A few minutes before 10:00 that night, the god-king, brokenhearted and disguised as a common soldier, left his palace for the last time. He was twenty-three years old.

Along with a small escort, he made his way undetected through the throng, out of Lhasa, and across a nearby river. There he met his entourage, including his immediate family. Together they began a three-week trek to freedom—north of Lhasa, then circling back southeast toward the Indian border. As they slowly progressed toward exile, news caught up to them about the brutal Chinese reaction. Having crushed the revolt by turning much of

The Dalai Lama (middle, riding a white horse) flees from Tibet into India through the rugged Himalayan Mountains.

China's Attitude Toward Tibet

"Tibet has been an inseparable part of China since ancient times. The peaceful liberation of Tibet, the driving out of the imperialist aggressor forces from Tibet, the democratic reform and abolition of theocratic feudal serfdom in Tibet were significant parts of the Chinese people's national democratic revolution against imperialism and feudalism in modern history." This is the official opinion from Beijing in regards to Tibet, published in an article from the *Xinhua News Agency* dated March 2, 2009.

As far as the revolt that followed the Dalai Lama's departure from Tibet in 1959, Xinhua sees it this way: "The '17-Article Agreement' [the "Seventeen-Point Agreement for the Peaceful Liberation of Tibet"] acknowledged the necessity of reforming the social system of Tibet, and stressed that 'the local government of Tibet should carry out reform voluntarily.' However, in consideration of the special circumstances of Tibet, the Central People's Government adopted a circumscribed attitude toward the reform. With great patience, tolerance and sincerity, it made efforts to persuade and waited for the local upper ruling strata of Tibet to carry out reform voluntarily. Instigated and supported by imperialist forces, however, some people in the upper strata, despite the ever-growing demand of the people for democratic reform, were totally opposed to reform and proclaimed their determination never to carry it out. In an attempt to perpetuate feudal serfdom under theocracy, these people publicly abandoned the '17-Article Agreement' and brazenly staged an all-out armed rebellion on March 10, 1959. In order to safeguard the unity of the nation and the basic interests of the Tibetan people, the Central People's Government and the Tibetan people took decisive measures to quell the rebellion. Meanwhile, a vigorous democratic reform were [sic] carried out on a massive scale in Tibet to overthrow Tibet's feudal serfdom system under theocracy and liberate about one million serfs and slaves, ushering in a new era with the people becoming their own masters."

"Full Text: Fifty Years of Democratic Reform in Tibet (1)." *Xinhua News Agency*. March 2, 2009. Accessed on HighBeam Research website August 5, 2009. http://www.highbeam.com/doc/1P2-19953430.html.

Lhasa into a smoldering ruin, the Chinese realized they had been outwitted. Immediately, they announced to the world that the Dalai Lama had been kidnapped.

Traveling by foot and on mules, the Dalai Lama's group slowly moved southeast, guarded by a force of three hundred resistance fighters. Plagued by high mountain passes, bad weather, and disease, the Dalai Lama and his party crossed into the sparsely populated, heavily wooded Assam Province of India on March 31, 1959. Before leaving Tibet, the Dalai Lama released his armed escort, sending them to join the desperate fight for Lhasa. Remaining were eighty physically and mentally exhausted refugees. The Dalai Lama had fallen ill with dysentery, so attendants placed him on the broad back of a *dzomo*. Borne atop this humble yet typically Tibetan beast of burden, he traveled the final miles to freedom.

Chapter 4

India and Beyond

Once the Dalai Lama left Tibet, he was faced with the difficult task of telling the world what had happened in his country and trying to obtain aid for his people. He also had to counter China's propaganda broadcasts that he had been kidnapped. His most pressing need, however, was to secure housing and food for his party and for Tibetans who would follow him into exile. He turned to the Indian government, and they did not disappoint him. In fact, India eventually took in more than a hundred thousand Tibetans, housed them, fed them, put them to work, and established special Tibetan schools for their children. Tibetan Buddhist monasteries were also built in India and Nepal.

For the first few years, the Dalai Lama stayed in India, traveling across the country to visit his people in refugee camps. Then, he decided to take his message to a wider audience. He traveled around the world and did what no other dalai lama had ever done. He spoke to large gatherings of non-Buddhists about issues that affected not only his occupied nation but the world at large. For this, he became one of the world's most admired and respected figures, fulfilling the Nechung Oracle's prophesy that he would "shine in the West."

India Offers a New Life

The Indian government, having earlier voted to provide sanctuary to the Dalai Lama and his entourage, sent representatives to meet them when they crossed into India on March 30, 1959. They carried with them a telegram from Prime Minister Nehru: "My colleagues and I welcome you and send greetings on your safe arrival in India. We shall be happy to afford the necessary facilities to you, your family and entourage to reside in India. The people of India, who hold you in great veneration, will no doubt accord their traditional respect to your personage."[27] The representatives were also sent to escort the refugees to Bomdila, a large city a week's journey from the border. There the travelers spent ten days recuperating from their ordeal.

After he had fully recovered, the Dalai Lama went to Foothills, a small outpost near the town of Tezpur, India. From there he and his party were to go by train to Mussoorie, a former British hill station near Delhi, some 1,500 miles (2,414km) away, where the Indian government had provided a house for him. Before leaving for Mussoorie, he decided to make a statement to the press

The Dalai Lama (right) discusses the Chinese atrocities in Tibet while speaking at a mass press conference in India.

about what happened in Tibet and why he decided to leave. *Time* later reported on his news conference:

> Out of the station wagon stepped the 23-year-old Dalai Lama, God-King of Tibet, wearing a beatific smile but sniffling slightly from a head cold. His eyes were bright and warm behind orange-rimmed glasses, and he wore the simple russet gown of a high lama, with no special marks of rank. Surrounded by his mother, brother and sister and by Cabinet ministers and officials, the Dalai Lama smiled and nodded as he moved slowly by the news photographers. . . . [During the press conference,] he stated "categorically," in the third-person style expected of a god, that he left Lhasa and Tibet and came to India "of his own will and not under duress," and said that his "quite arduous" escape was only possible "due to the loyalty and affectionate support of his Tibetan people." . . . [He] bluntly accused the Red Chinese of destroying a large number of monasteries, killing lamas and forcing monks and officials into labor camps. He had left Lhasa in fear of his own life, said the Dalai Lama, when the Communists opened fire on his Norbulingka palace with mortar shells.[28]

After releasing his statement, the Dalai Lama and his party boarded their train for Mussoorie. All along the route, tens of thousands of Indians lined the tracks, waving and shouting their welcome, "*Dalai Lama Ki Jai! Dalai Lama Zinda-bad!'* ('Hail to the Dalai Lama! Long live the Dalai Lama!')."[29]

Dealing with the Press and the Refugees

In Mussoorie the Dalai Lama was escorted to Birla House. Once settled, he heard a radio broadcast from China's *Xinhua* news agency that claimed his Tezpur statement had been full of lies and had obviously been written by someone else. He issued a second statement, confirming the Tezpur statement was authentic.

Almost as soon as he arrived in Mussoorie, news reached the Dalai Lama that a large number of Tibetan refugees had begun

Tibetan refugees forced to leave their homeland arrive at a makeshift camp in Missamari, India.

arriving in India. He sent representatives to greet them at camps that had been hastily set up by the Indian government. Nehru visited Birla House, and they discussed what needed to be done for the refugees. They also discussed how Tibetan children should be educated to prepare them for life outside Tibet.

According to the Dalai Lama, Nehru told him that he expected Tibetan refugees to "be guests of India for the foreseeable future" and that education of the children had to be a top priority. He also insisted that they have separate schools and that a special section be established within the Indian Ministry of Education for Tibetan education. He added that the Indian government would bear the expense for the schools. "Finally, he cautioned me that, whilst it was very important for our children to be brought up with a thorough knowledge of their own history and culture, it was vital that they should be conversant with the ways of the modern world. I agreed wholeheartedly. For that reason, he said, we would be wise to use English as our medium of instruction, for 'it is the international language of the future.'"[30]

On June 20, 1959, the Dalai Lama called another press conference to speak out more strongly against Chinese aggression in Tibet. More than one hundred reporters from all over the world attended. He again repudiated the Seventeen-Point Agreement. He outlined in detail what he had heard about the treatment of his people by Chinese troops. By this time he had received reports from countless refugees about what they had seen or suffered, and he shared some of those stories with the world press. The International Commission of Jurists, an independent association representing judges, law professors, and lawyers from fifty countries, published a report that year that verified the Dalai Lama's claims of China's crimes against Tibet. Besides countless specific charges of aggression, the report accused China of genocide, the attempted annihilation of Tibet's Buddhist population. They called genocide "the gravest crime of which any person or nation can be accused . . . the intent to destroy, in whole or in part, a national, ethnical, racial, or religious group."[31]

Changes

In addition to addressing the world press, the Dalai Lama continued reforming his own government by making it more democratic. He also gave weekly audiences to a wide variety of people. He did away with much of the strict protocol that had always been demanded of people who met him. He created new departments in the Tibetan government in exile—offices of information, education, religious affairs, security, and economic affairs—and encouraged women to take part in government more than they had done in Tibet.

The Dalai Lama felt it was vital to the future of his people to make use of the world forum of the United Nations. He wrote to governments asking for assistance in addressing the United Nations. Two countries, Malaya and Ireland, sponsored a resolution that later passed in favor of Tibet, although the resolution accomplished little.

In the spring of 1960, India announced it wanted to move the Dalai Lama and his government in exile to the city of Dharamsala, a more suitable and more permanent location, and just a day's journey from India's capital. The Dalai Lama sent a representative to visit the site. He declared it acceptable. On March 10, 1960, the one-year anniversary of the Tibetan People's Uprising, the Dalai Lama issued a statement to all the Tibetan people, in Tibet and in refugee camps in India. He stressed the need for a long-range view of what had happened. He urged Tibetans in exile to focus on the continuation of Tibetan culture.

The exiled Dalai Lama sits inside his home at Dharamsala, India.

McLeod Ganj

The Dalai Lama's residence is located in northern India, in the state of Himachal Pradesh, high in the foothills of the Himalayas. The white stucco house, along with numerous outbuildings, overlooks a broad valley and the village of McLeod Ganj, a former British outpost several miles from the city of Dharamsala, India. The site once housed the British divisional commissioner. It is a relatively modest house, set in woodlands, and furnished simply. It bears little resemblance to the plush throne rooms and apartments of Lhasa's Potala Palace or the Norbulingka, other than having a spectacular view of snow-capped mountains.

The Dalai Lama originally shared his new home with his mother and two Lhasa Apso dogs that admirers had given him. (One of those admirers was Tenzin Norgay, the Nepalese mountaineer who had accompanied Sir Edmund

 Hillary on his historic climb to the top of Mount Everest in 1953.) The dogs, Sangye and Tashi, provided loyal companionship and amused everyone who came in contact with them.

The Dalai Lama stands in front of stunning mountain scenery near his home in Dharamsala, India.

Further Changes

In their first ten years in exile, Tibetans, including the Dalai Lama, underwent radical changes. They left the nation of their birth, their feudal form of government, much of the strict protocol associated with their leader, their livelihoods, sometimes members of their families, and many of their possessions.

During those years the Dalai Lama also made additional changes to his government. He inaugurated what today is called Bhoe Mimang Chetui Lhenkhang, meaning the Assembly of Tibetan People's Deputies, a legislative body of freely elected officials similar to a house of parliament. In 1961 this assembly published a draft constitution for Tibet, based on Buddhist philosophy, democratic ideals, and the United Nations' Universal Declaration of Human Rights. To the shock of many Tibetans, the document featured a clause that allowed the assembly to depose the Dalai Lama if two-thirds of the representatives concurred. The Dalai Lama himself had suggested the clause and later insisted that it remain in the document.

In 1968 the Dalai Lama moved to new quarters, this one called Thekchen Choeling Monastery, still in the Dharamsala area. His new home was located in a newly built compound with larger buildings to house his private office, the department that handles the Dalai Lama's personal financial affairs, and the Indian Security Office, charged with protecting him. Another building provides a location for public audiences.

World Travels

Beginning in 1967, the Dalai Lama traveled to other countries, first to discuss religious issues with other Buddhists but later to spread his message about conditions in Tibet, his attempts to negotiate with China, and eventually about issues relating to the world at large. During that first flight out of India, on his way to Japan and Thailand, he became disheartened when he saw a U.S. Air Force B-52 bomber he knew must be on its way to bomb a target in North Vietnam during the Vietnam War. He realized the plane was carrying death and destruction to human beings on the ground, people who were just like him. He was further dismayed when he realized, even at 30,000 feet (9,144m) above the Earth, he could not escape seeing evidence of the destruction mankind was capable of inflicting.

In 1973 the Dalai Lama made his first trip to the West. He went to Europe and Scandinavia, visiting eleven countries in six weeks. This trip gave him the opportunity to see Heinrich Harrer again. It also gave him the chance to personally thank individuals, organizations, and governments who had helped Tibetan refugees. In Rome he met with Pope Paul VI at the Vatican. In Switzerland he visited Tibetan refugee children who had been adopted by Swiss families. In Holland he met with a rabbi who had survived the Holocaust. In England he was quite taken with how much the British people sympathized with Tibet's situation.

He had to wait to visit the United States, however. Negotiations between the United States and China, he was told, were too

During his extensive travels through Europe in the 1970s and 1980s, the Dalai Lama met with high-ranking political and religious leaders like Pope John Paul II.

delicate. His visit might be considered "inconvenient." In 1979, though, during President Jimmy Carter's administration, the Dalai Lama visited America for the first time:

> On arrival in New York [City] . . . I was immediately impressed by an atmosphere of liberty. The people I met seemed very friendly and open and relaxed. But at the same time, I could not help noticing how dirty and untidy some parts of the city were. I was also very sorry to see so many tramps and homeless people taking shelter in doorways. It amazed me that there could be any beggars in this vastly rich and prosperous land. . . . Another surprise was to discover that although, like many Easterners, I held the view that the US was the champion of freedom actually few people had any knowledge of the fate of Tibet. Now, as I have come to know the country better, I have begun to see that, in some ways, the American political system does not live up to its own ideals.[32]

While in New York City, he spoke at a prayer service in Saint Patrick's Cathedral, an "extraordinary interreligious festival," according to a *Time* report. "The Dalai Lama, 44, was surrounded by a group of Protestant, Armenian, Catholic and Jewish clergy. To lend a Tibetan air to the proceedings, a group of monks clanged cymbals and blew traditional horns."[33]

On his twenty-two-city/seven-week tour, he met with groups of American Buddhists. In Washington he spoke to congressmen and members of the Senate Foreign Relations Committee. Mostly, he spoke on university campuses across the country to crowds of young people eager to hear about a culture that did not glorify materialism.

The Dalai Lama's Message to the World

When writing about his travels, the Dalai Lama reveals his underlying philosophy—that all humans are basically alike:

> Since those first visits to different parts of the world, I have been back many times. Especially, I welcome the opportunity offered by travel to meet and talk with people from different

Tibetan Children's Village

Fourteen days after moving to Dharamsala, the Dalai Lama opened the first nursery for Tibetan orphans. He appointed his older sister Tsering Dolma to head the operation, and before long, hundreds of children were living there. This first effort eventually led to the creation of the Tibetan Children's Village (TCV), an organization with branches throughout the refugee settlements in India. Today, the TCV houses and educates thousands of Tibetan children and serves as a model for refugee communities around the world. Before it became so widespread and successful, however, it faced severe overcrowding.

Conditions became so crowded at the first nursery—with as many as 120 children sharing a room and sometimes sleeping 5 or 6 to a bed—that the Dalai Lama contacted the government of Switzerland about the possibility of sending children there to be adopted by Swiss families. The Swiss government agreed. They also agreed to the Dalai Lama's stipulation that the children, as far as possible, be given the opportunity to study and maintain their cultural heritage. Older students were sent to Switzerland to study, and one thousand adult refugees also made that European nation their home away from home.

walks of life—some poor, some rich, some well educated, some ill educated, some who are religious, many who are not. So far, I have received only support for my belief that wherever you go, people everywhere are basically the same, despite certain superficial differences. They all, like myself, seek happiness: no one wants suffering. Furthermore, everyone appreciates affection and at the same time has the potential for showing affection to others. With this in mind, I have found that friendship and understanding can develop.[34]

Of the West, he says he is impressed with "its energy and creativity and hunger for knowledge." However, he says that West-

The Dalai Lama speaks to a crowd at New York's Central Park. He has visited the United States on several occasions and always looks forward to talking with people from different walks of life.

erners tend to think "in terms of 'black and white' and 'either, or', which ignores the facts of interdependence and relativity. [Westerners] have a tendency to lose sight of the grey areas which inevitably exist between two points of view."[35]

Since he first left India, the Dalai Lama has visited more than sixty-five countries on six continents. He has been to the United States thirty-five times. He has shared his philosophy and ideas with countless millions of people through public speeches, books, and teachings. Whenever he is asked to speak, he says he always approaches the task on three levels. First, he speaks as a human being, so he can discuss our responsibilities toward each other and for the planet on which we live. Second, he addresses his listeners as a Buddhist monk, trying to bring harmony and understanding among believers of different faiths. Third, he speaks as a Tibetan, about the country he loves, the people and culture he cherishes, and its need for justice and protection.

Chapter 5

Decades of Change

I n 1959 a Chinese threat against the Dalai Lama led to a Lhasa protest. Hoping to avoid bloodshed, he fled into exile, and more than 150,000 Tibetans have since followed him. Unfortunately, this action did not prevent bloodshed. Some reports say that as many as one million Tibetans have died since that year as a direct result of the Chinese takeover of Tibet. World newspapers corroborated those claims. Sources told the *Washington Post*, for example, that China's intent was to eradicate the Buddhist religion, dismantle the Tibetan government, and attempt to indoctrinate Tibetan children into embracing Communism. Reports verified that the Chinese went so far as to forcibly remove hundreds of children from their homes in Tibet and relocate them to Chinese orphanages for that purpose. In the decades following the Dalai Lama's escape to India, much has happened, but the restoration of Tibet's independence has not.

In 1979, twenty years after his escape, the Dalai Lama visited the United States for the first time and was awarded honorary doctorate degrees in humanities, Buddhist philosophy, and divinity. In that year, too, Tibet's government in exile made its first contact with the People's Republic of China, but little came of it. Incidentally, 1979 was also the year that China's capital stopped being called Peking by the West and became known as Beijing.

In 1989 the Dalai Lama was awarded the Nobel Peace Prize in Oslo, Norway. In 1999 he addressed an enthusiastic crowd of two hundred thousand people in New York City's Central Park. In 2009 Tibet is still under Chinese control, the Chinese government is still opposed to direct negotiations with the Dalai Lama, and, at the age of seventy-four, he is still a refugee, living in exile away from six million Tibetans who want to see him come home.

1979: First Contact with China

On August 2, 1979, the Dalai Lama dispatched a delegation of five members of the Tibetan government in exile to China and then to Tibet. These delegates were carefully chosen to be as objective as possible, with knowledge both of Tibet before Chinese rule and of the modern world. Each region of Tibet was represented. The Dalai Lama's older brother, Lobsang Samten, who had long since renounced his monastic vows, was one of the delegates.

After two weeks in Beijing, the group entered Tibet through the Dalai Lama's home province of Amdo. Everywhere they went, they were mobbed by crowds of Tibetans, eager to receive blessings and hear news of their beloved leader. This form of open devotion to the Dalai Lama had been expressly forbidden by Chinese officials, but Tibetans defied these orders and greeted the delegates with ecstatic fervor. In Lhasa, where Chinese officials had assured Beijing no such demonstrations would take place, thousands flooded the streets for a chance to touch one of the Dalai Lama's representatives or to catch a glimpse of them.

The representatives, after four months touring every corner of Tibet, returned to Dharamsala with hundreds of rolls of film, hours of recorded interviews, and volumes of printed materials documenting what they had seen. They also brought more than seven thousand letters, the first exchange of mail between Tibetans and family members in exile in twenty years. Their assessment of the "new Tibet" was almost entirely negative. They reported evidence of famine, starvation, and public executions, mass imprisonments, destroyed monasteries, and forced labor camps. The Dalai Lama was sickened by their report.

They noted some improvements in Tibet's economy, but most of those benefits went to China or Chinese settlers in Tibet, not

His Holiness, the fourteenth Dalai Lama, leads a discussion in 1979. That same year, he dispatched a group of delegates to report on the state of Tibet's people and the Chinese occupation.

to Tibetans. The improvements had come at a terrible cost. The country's economic output had increased, but so had erosion due to deforestation and short-sighted farming practices, the almost complete annihilation of Tibet's abundant wildlife, and high taxation.

Two subsequent delegations were sent in 1980. The first, made up of young people, was greeted by Tibetans in much the same way as the earlier group. When public demonstrations began this time, though, Chinese officials "accused the delegates of inciting the masses to acts of defiance and expelled the delegation from Tibet for endangering the 'unity of the Motherland.'"[36] Another delegation, made up of educators, was allowed to survey the country's educational system. It returned to Dharamsala to report that, despite improvements in the education of Tibet's children, the school system was used almost exclusively to indoctrinate young Tibetans to Communist ideals.

1987: The Five-Point Peace Plan and Demonstrations

The Dalai Lama visited the United States in 1979, 1981, and 1984. Each time, U.S. officials and citizens expressed the desire to do something concrete for Tibet. In 1987 the Dalai Lama was awarded the Albert Schweitzer Humanitarian Award by America's Human Behavior Foundation. He also received an invitation to address the Human Rights Caucus of the U.S. Congress. He delivered his address on September 21, 1987. What he outlined for the future of Tibet became known as the Five-Point Peace Plan.

Although his address took place in a small committee room before only a half-dozen members of the caucus, it was deemed historic. He rescinded Tibet's former demands for independence and called instead for all of Tibet to be designated a zone of *Ahimsa* (a Hindi term for peace and nonviolence). He called for the cessation of Chinese immigration into Tibet, demanded "respect for the Tibetan people's fundamental human rights and democratic freedoms," "restoration and protection of Tibet's natural environment," an end to China's policy of using Tibet for "the production of nuclear weapons and dumping of nuclear waste," and the establishment of meaningful dialogue between representatives of Tibet's government in exile and China about "the future status of Tibet and relations between Tibetan and Chinese peoples."[37]

His abandonment of demands for Tibetan independence caused quite a stir in China and in the rest of the world. The Dalai Lama called instead for autonomy for Tibet within China, subject to the approval of the Tibetan people. In exchange for allowing Tibetans to have control over most internal affairs of the region and for China's removal of its settlers from Tibet, the Dalai Lama offered to allow Tibet to remain a part of China.

An activist in India wearing anti-Chinese slogans particpates in a protest rally calling for Tibet's independence.

American civil rights lawyer John Ackerly (right) witnessed the horrifying Chinese police action against Tibetan protestors in 1987 and summarily cofounded the International Campaign for Tibet organization.

The government in Beijing denounced the Five-Point Peace Plan, calling it a sham and a thinly disguised declaration of independence. Protests sprang up in Lhasa because of China's response and by people who disagreed with autonomy rather than complete independence. Thousands took to the streets. Chinese authorities responded harshly, sending armed police to break up the demonstrations.

One witness to the police action was John Ackerly, an American civil rights lawyer visiting Tibet on vacation. In a 2009 letter to members of the International Campaign for Tibet, an organization he cofounded after returning from that trip, he describes what he witnessed on the streets of Lhasa on October 1, 1987:

> The horror of repression is etched on my mind forever: Chinese police firing into unarmed crowds. Monks, teenagers and children gunned down. Dozens of Tibetans at the Jokhang Temple walking towards a line of Chinese troops who opened fire on them. A boy bleeding to death as my friend, a doctor, held him, unable to save him. The day began with a peaceful protest by about 20 monks. It ended senselessly, with more than 10 Tibetans dead, and scores who were badly injured but could not go to the hospital for fear of being arrested for being at the demonstration. We tried to get medical supplies to them, and maybe saved some lives, but others died of infection while hiding from the police. During that deadly day, Tibetans begged me to take pictures and show them to the outside world. And so I became a witness to a brutal occupation that had been going on unseen for decades. We were arrested, and interrogated for several days, but ultimately managed to get out of Tibet with the film, which I still show today.[38]

According to the Dalai Lama, as a result of that one day's demonstration, more than two thousand Tibetans were imprisoned. Other demonstrations followed, and despite worldwide coverage of their atrocities and a call by several Western governments for the Chinese to respect Tibetan human rights, the Chinese government dismissed the criticism, saying the disturbances were an internal matter.

On June 15, 1988, the Dalai Lama addressed the European Parliament in Strasbourg, France, stressing his previous peace plan. Again the Chinese reaction was negative. The speech was denounced and the European Parliament severely criticized. Months later, in 1989, demonstrations by Chinese students in Beijing's Tiananmen Square were met with violence and repression. The Dalai Lama watched these demonstrations with interest and optimism and applauded the courage of those students.

1989: The Nobel Peace Prize

The same year demonstrations were taking place in China, martial law had been declared in Tibet as a result of protests. Ironically, it was the year the Human Rights Foundation in Washington, D.C., voted to present the Dalai Lama the Raoul Wallenberg Congressional Human Rights Award. It was also the year he received an even more prestigious award. The Norwegian Nobel Committee announced that its Nobel Prize for Peace for 1989 was to go to the Dalai Lama.

The committee stated it wanted to

emphasise that the Dalai Lama in his struggle for the liberation of Tibet has consistently opposed the use of violence. He has instead advocated peaceful solutions based upon tolerance and mutual respect in order to preserve the historical and cultural heritage of his people. The Dalai Lama has developed his philosophy of peace from a great reverence of all things living and upon the concept of universal responsibility embracing all mankind as well as nature.[39]

The Dalai Lama later wrote, "Although the news did not matter much to me personally, I realised that it would mean a great deal to the people of Tibet, for it was they who were the real 'winners' of the prize. My own satisfaction derived from what I saw as international recognition of the value of compassion, forgiveness, and love."[40] He received the award on December 10, 1989, in Oslo, Norway.

Nobel Prize laureates Dalai Lama (left) and Poland's Lech Walesa (right) are applauded.

In his Nobel lecture, delivered the following day, the Dalai Lama summarized his Five-Point Peace Plan, discussed the status of Tibet under Chinese occupation, and shared with listeners his philosophy of peace:

Peace, in the sense of the absence of war, is of little value to someone who is dying of hunger or cold. It will not remove the pain of torture inflicted on a prisoner of conscience. It does not comfort those who have lost their loved ones in floods caused by senseless deforestation in a neighboring country. Peace can only last where human rights are respected, where the people are fed, and where individuals and nations are free.[41]

1999: Another Landmark Visit to the United States

In 1999 the Dalai Lama was invited by the Gere Foundation and the Tibet Center to come to the United States and conduct a series of teachings. American actor Richard Gere had met the Dalai Lama in Dharamsala in 1980 and had become one of his biggest supporters. During this visit, the Dalai Lama gave three days of formal teachings at the Beacon Theatre on Manhattan's Upper West Side before three thousand people. He then agreed to conduct a more public and informal session in Central Park.

Organizers were hoping that fifteen thousand to twenty thousand people would attend. At 11:00 AM on Sunday, August 15, when Richard Gere introduced him, the Dalai Lama stepped onto the flower-covered stage, bowed to the crowd, sat on a simple wooden chair, and delivered a two-hour lecture in English. The crowd in the East Meadow was estimated at two hundred thousand. A massive

American actor Richard Gere (right), a serious supporter of His Holiness, invited the Dalai Lama (left) to share his teachings in New York City in 1999.

sound system and video monitors carried his message of peace to far-distant corners of the crowd.

2007: The U.S. Congressional Gold Medal

On October 17, 2007, months before the city of Beijing and the Chinese people were to host the 2008 Summer Olympics, the Dalai Lama once again visited Washington, D.C. He addressed the entire U.S. Congress, the president and first lady, and other dignitaries. The occasion was the presentation of the U.S. Congressional Gold Medal. Introducing the Dalai Lama to the assembly, the late congressman Tom Lantos of California, the only Holocaust survivor to serve in the U.S. Congress, said,

What accounts for the rise of this humble Buddhist monk from near-obscurity to the global phenomenon that he has become is not lobbies. It is not economic power. It is not political influence. It is moral authority. At a moment in world history when nothing is in as short supply as moral authority, this humble Buddhist monk has an inexhaustible supply. And this accounts for the respect, the admiration, the love that people have for him across the globe.[42]

While the Dalai Lama was addressing Congress, thanking the United States for its strong support and commenting on China's rise in economic power and hosting the Olympic Games, two Tibetans were risking their lives to reveal the true story of Tibet's occupation. Dhondup Wangchen, a Tibetan filmmaker, with the help of Jigme Gyatso, a monk from the Amdo Labrang monastery, traveled across the Tibetan plateau in 2007 and made a documentary

House Speaker Nancy Pelosi's Introduction

"With this Gold Medal, we affirm the special relationship between the United States and the Dalai Lama. It is a relationship that began with a gold watch. As a boy, the Dalai Lama enjoyed science and mechanics. Knowing this, President Franklin Roosevelt gave the very young Dalai Lama a watch showing the phases of the moon and the days of the week. The Dalai Lama described the gold watch as magnificent and even took it with him when he fled Tibet in 1959. His Holiness still uses the watch today and his teaching about the connection between science and religion is an inspiring part of his message. . . . Your Holiness: you bring lustre to this award, and a challenge to the conscience of the world."

Office of His Holiness the Dalai Lama, "Speech by Speaker Nancy Pelosi." www.dalai lama.com/page.203.htm.

later released under the title *Leaving Fear Behind*. At great personal risk, they filmed ordinary Tibetans sharing their feelings about the Dalai Lama, China, and the Olympic Games.

After the film was released, on March 10, 2008—the forty-ninth anniversary of the Dalai Lama's departure from Tibet—Dhondup Wangchen was arrested. He is still in detention in a secret Chinese prison. Jigme Gyatso was also arrested, released, and then rearrested—for sharing his story with the International Campaign for Tibet. His tales of torture at the hands of Chinese officials horrified listeners. He, too, is still in prison.

2009: Fiftieth Anniversary and a Look to the Future

On March 10, 2009, the Dalai Lama issued his annual statement on the anniversary of the Tibetan uprising that led him to flee his homeland:

> Today is the fiftieth anniversary of the Tibetan people's peaceful uprising against Communist China's repression in Tibet. Since last March widespread peaceful protests have erupted across the whole of Tibet. Most of the participants were youths born and brought up after 1959, who have not seen or experienced a free Tibet. However, the fact that they were driven by a firm conviction to serve the cause of Tibet that has continued from generation to generation is indeed a matter of pride. It will serve as a source of inspiration for those in the international community who take a keen interest in the issue of Tibet. We pay tribute and offer our prayers for all those who died, were tortured and suffered tremendous hardships, including during the crisis last year [before the Beijing Olympics], for the cause of Tibet since our struggle began.[43]

Three days later, the Chinese press issued its usual denunciation of the Dalai Lama and his annual message to the world. In the release, it called him "a politician in monk's robes," "chief rebel," "an ill-intentioned politician who promoted separatist movements," and "fodder [in the West] for sound-bites, photo-

The Foundation for Universal Responsibility

With the prize money awarded by the Nobel Committee, the Dalai Lama established the Foundation for Universal Responsibility, with administrative headquarters in New Delhi, India. The foundation's goal is to promote "universal responsibility in a manner that respects and encourages a diversity of beliefs and practices; promotes and devises strategies to transform this commitment into an instrument of social change for personal happiness."

The foundation's mission statement continues by saying it "brings together people of different faiths, persuasions, professions and nationalities. It does not promote an individual or idea; instead, it seeks to bring together insights and techniques that will further its goals. To the Dalai Lama, it represents a reaching out beyond his role as the pre-eminent Buddhist monk and transcends the political agenda of a free Tibet."

His Holiness the XIV Dalai Lama, *The Heart of Compassion: A Practical Approach to a Meaningful Life*. India: Full Circle/Foundation for Universal Responsibility, 2001; Twin Lakes, WI: Lotus Press, 2002, pp. vi–vii.

ops, and newspaper front-page slots."[44] According to a February 18, 2009, *Huffington Post* report, "The Chinese government is hailing March 2009 as the 50th anniversary of 'democratic reform' in Tibet."[45] According to a *Christian Science Monitor* report, "some senior [Chinese] officials have taken to referring to the Dalai Lama as 'a beast' set on snatching Tibet away from Chinese sovereignty. The stepped up vitriol, such as a recent editorial in the official *Tibet Daily* calling on people to 'firmly crush the savage aggression of the Dalai clique,' makes the possibility of the Dalai Lama's return seem quite remote at the moment."[46]

Despite China's longstanding rhetoric about the Dalai Lama and its pressure on world powers to drop the Tibet issue, several countries, including the United States, continue to press for a solution.

On March 11, 2009, U.S. president Barack Obama signed an appropriations bill with dozens of provisions dealing with Tibet, including funding a Tibet section in the U.S. Embassy in Beijing until the Chinese government allows a U.S. consulate to be established in Lhasa. On March 16 President Obama and the U.S. House of Representatives again stated in a resolution that they expect Beijing to negotiate, despite having been warned repeatedly by China to drop the issue.

For more than a decade the Dalai Lama has talked about retirement, or partial retirement. At seventy-four, his optimism about China relenting and allowing any measure of autonomy for Tibet in his lifetime has waned. But he has not lost heart. As a Buddhist, he believes that eventually the law of karma will bring justice for the Tibetan people. Karma is the law of cause and effect, played out in multiple lifetimes—that anything a person does, says, or thinks that is harmful in one life will have to be counteracted in a subsequent lifetime.

His biggest fear in 2009 is that the Tibetan culture, despite his best efforts, may be on the brink of extinction. Today more Chinese live in Tibet than Tibetans, and he fears Tibetans may soon become a curious and perhaps picturesque, insignificant minority in their own country. At his age, the Dalai Lama also believes China may be stubbornly refusing to negotiate directly with him because they are waiting for him to die. He feels they mistakenly believe that, once he is out of the picture, Tibetans will lose their will to gain independence or autonomy. He knows, however, that the Tibetan people will wait for his reincarnation to make itself known. The struggle will continue.

The Dalai Lama points out that in 2007 China issued new rules about the selection and identification of the next god-king. It has declared that any reincarnation must be approved by China's cabinet. He, on the other hand, has stated many times that

> if I die in the near future, and the Tibetan people want another reincarnation, a 15th Dalai Lama, while we are still outside Tibet, my reincarnation will definitely appear outside Tibet. Because the very purpose of the incarnation is to fulfill the work that has been started by the previous life.

[Therefore] the reincarnation of the 14th Dalai Lama, logically, will not be a reincarnation that disturbs, or is an obstacle to, that work. Quite clear, isn't it?[47]

When his death and reincarnation occur, two Dalai Lamas may emerge, one sanctioned by China, which the people of Tibet will not recognize, and another, born outside Tibet, in a free country.

As to the future of the world, the Dalai Lama is ever hopeful. Despite terrorism and continuing wars, he sees evidence that mankind has made some progress toward a more peaceful, happier

Exiled Tibetans protest the Chinese occupation of their homeland during a march marking the fiftieth anniversary of the Tibetan uprising and the Dalai Lama's flight to India.

The Dalai Lama's Acceptance Speech

In his acceptance speech for the Nobel Peace Prize, delivered at the University of Oslo, Norway, on December 10, 1989, the Dalai Lama stated:

I feel honored, humbled and deeply moved that you should give this important prize to a simple monk from Tibet. I am no one special. But I believe the prize is a recognition of the true value of altruism, love, compassion and non-violence which I try to practice, in accordance with the teachings of the Buddha and the great sages of India and Tibet. I accept the prize with profound gratitude on behalf of the oppressed everywhere and for all those who struggle for freedom and work for world peace. I accept it as a tribute to the man who founded the modern tradition of non-violent action for change Mahatma Gandhi whose life taught and inspired me. And, of course, I accept it on behalf of the

six million Tibetan people, my brave countrymen and women inside Tibet, who have suffered and continue to suffer so much.

Office of His Holiness the Dalai Lama, "Nobel Peace Prize Acceptance Speech," December 10, 1989. www.dalailama .com/page.118.htm.

Following the Dalai Lama's Nobel Prize for Peace in 1989, Tibetan prisoners created small symbols like this one to celebrate the prestigious award.

world. Of course, as a Buddhist, he takes a long-range look at things. Still, he remains optimistic. Howard C. Cutler, a psychologist who cowrote *The Art of Happiness: A Handbook for Living* with the Dalai Lama in 1998, says this about the fourteenth dalai lama—the "simple monk":

> As his message unfolded, it became increasingly clear that his beliefs are not based on blind faith or religious dogma but rather on sound reasoning and direct experience. His understanding of the human mind and behavior is based on a lifetime of study. His views are rooted in a tradition that dates back over twenty-five hundred years yet is tempered by common sense and a sophisticated understanding of modern problems. His appreciation of contemporary issues has been forged as a result of his unique position as a world figure, which has allowed him to travel the world many times, exposing himself to many different cultures and people from all walks of life, exchanging ideas with top scientists and religious and political leaders. What ultimately emerges is a wise approach to dealing with human problems that is at once optimistic and realistic.[48]

The Dalai Lama's compassion, philosophy, and optimism is best summarized by a short prayer he has recited countless times at the end of teachings and speeches around the world:

> For as long as space endures,
> And for as long as living beings remain,
> Until then may I, too, abide
> To dispel the misery of the world.[49]

Notes

Introduction: A Simple Monk

1. Quoted in Office of His Holiness the Dalai Lama, "Speech by Speaker Nancy Pelosi." www.dalailama.com/page.201.htm.
2. Tenzin Gyatso, the Fourteenth Dalai Lama of Tibet, *Freedom in Exile: The Autobiography of the Dalai Lama*. New York: HarperCollins, 1990, p. xiii.

Chapter 1: Rising from Obscurity

3. Tenzin Gyatso, *Freedom in Exile*, p. 3.
4. Tenzin Gyatso, *Freedom in Exile*, p. 7.
5. Quoted in Tom Morgan, ed., *A Simple Monk: Writings on His Holiness the Dalai Lama*. Novato, CA: New World Library, 2001, p. 23.
6. Quoted in Morgan, *A Simple Monk*, p. 23.
7. Tenzin Gyatso, *Freedom in Exile*, p. 8.
8. Pico Iyer, "The God in Exile," *Time*, December 22, 1997. www.time.com/time/magazine/article/0,9171,987571.html.
9. Quoted in Morgan, *A Simple Monk*, p. 24.
10. Tenzin Gyatso, *Freedom in Exile*, p. 12.

Chapter 2: Life in Lhasa

11. Tenzin Gyatso, *Freedom in Exile*, p. 14.
12. Tenzin Gyatso, *Freedom in Exile*, p. 19.
13. Tenzin Gyatso, *Freedom in Exile*, p. 21.
14. Tenzin Gyatso, *Freedom in Exile*, pp. 27–28.
15. Heinrich Harrer, *Seven Years in Tibet*. Norwalk, CT: Easton, 2004, pp. 223–24.
16. Harrer, *Seven Years in Tibet*, pp. 279–80.
17. Tenzin Gyatso, *Freedom in Exile*, p. 53.

Chapter 3: Into Exile

18. Quoted in Tenzin Gyatso, *Freedom in Exile*, p. 63.
19. Tenzin Gyatso, *Freedom in Exile*, pp. 99–100.

20. Tenzin Gyatso, *Freedom in Exile*, p. 101.
21. Robert A.F. Thurman, "Hope for the Third Millennium," *A Simple Monk: Writings on His Holiness the Dalai Lama*. Novato, CA: New World Library, 2001, p. 104. Originally published in Robert A.F. Thurman, *Inner Revolution*. New York: Riverhead, 1998.
22. Tenzin Gyatso, *Freedom in Exile*, p. 104.
23. Tenzin Gyatso, *Freedom in Exile*, p. 105.
24. *Time*, "Buddha & the Reds," December 17, 1956. www.time.com/time/magazine/article/0,9171,867428,00.html.
25. Tenzin Gyatso, *Freedom in Exile*, p. 122.
26. His Holiness, the Dalai Lama of Tibet, *My Land and My People*. New York: McGraw-Hill, 1962, p. 173.

Chapter 4: India and Beyond

27. Quoted in Tenzin Gyatso, *Freedom in Exile*, p. 144.
28. *Time*, "God-King in Exile," April 27, 1959. www.time.com/time/magazine/article/0,9171,811038,00.html.
29. Tenzin Gyatso, *Freedom in Exile*, p. 145.
30. Tenzin Gyatso, *Freedom in Exile*, pp. 150–51.
31. His Holiness, the Dalai Lama of Tibet, *My Land and My People*, p. 223.
32. Tenzin Gyatso, *Freedom in Exile*, p. 198.
33. *Time*, "I Am a Human Being: A Monk," September 17, 1979. www.time.com/time/magazine/article/0,9171,920681,00.html.
34. Tenzin Gyatso, *Freedom in Exile*, p. 199.
35. Tenzin Gyatso, *Freedom in Exile*, p. 199.

Chapter 5: Decades of Change

36. Tenzin Gyatso, *Freedom in Exile*, p. 238.
37. Tenzin Gyatso, *Freedom in Exile*, pp. 247–48.
38. John Ackerly, letter to members of the International Campaign for Tibet seeking renewal of membership for 2009, International Campaign for Tibet. www.savetibet.org.
39. Quoted in His Holiness the XIV Dalai Lama, *The Heart of Compassion: A Practical Approach to a Meaningful Life*. India: Full Circle/Foundation for Universal Responsibility, 2001; Twin Lakes, WI: Lotus, 2002, pp. vi–vii.

40. Tenzin Gyatso, *Freedom in Exile*, p. 263.
41. Office of His Holiness the Dalai Lama, "The 14th Dalai Lama—Nobel Lecture," December 11, 1989. www.dalailama.com/page.120.htm.
42. Quoted in Office of His Holiness the Dalai Lama, "Speech by Congressman Mr. Tom Lantos," October 17, 2007. www.dalailama.com/page.205.htm.
43. Office of His Holiness the Dalai Lama, "March 10th Statement of H.H. the Dalai Lama," March 10, 2009. www.dalailama.com/page.350.htm.
44. Xinhua News Agency, "China Focus: An Enigmatic Paradox—How a Layman Sees the Dalai Lama (1)," HighBeam Research, 2009. www.highbeam.com/doc/1P2-20012510.html.
45. Rebecca Novick, "Why Tibetans Won't Come to the Party," *Huffington Post*. Posted February 18, 2009. International Campaign for Tibet, "Why Tibetans Won't Come to the Party," *Tibet Press Watch*, Spring 2009, p. 6.
46. Peter Ford, "In Exile 50 Years, Will the Dalai Lama Ever Return to Tibet?" *Christian Science Monitor*, March 10, 2009. www.highbeam.com/doc/1G1-195162634.html.
47. Quoted in Pico Iyer, "The God in Exile," *Time*, May 22, 1997. www.time.com/time/magazine/article/0,9171,987571,00.html.
48. His Holiness the Dalai Lama and Howard C. Cutler, *The Art of Happiness: A Handbook for Living*. New York: Riverhead, 1998, pp. 8–9.
49. Office of His Holiness the Dalai Lama, "The 14th Dalai Lama—Nobel Lecture."

Important Dates

December 17, 1933
Thirteenth dalai lama dies in Lhasa, Tibet, at age fifty-seven.

July 6, 1935
Lhamo Thondup, later identified as the fourteenth dalai lama, born in Taktser, Amdo, Tibet.

October 8, 1939
Procession carrying the Dalai Lama and his family enters Lhasa following a three-month journey from Amdo.

February 22, 1940
Enthronement ceremony at Potala Palace.

November 17, 1950
The Dalai Lama assumes full temporal (political) power after China's invasion of Tibet in 1949.

May 23, 1951
Seventeen-Point Agreement signed by Tibetan delegation in China, under duress.

July 1954–June 1955
The Dalai Lama visits China for peace talks. Meets with Mao Ze-dong and other Chinese leaders, including Chou En-Lai, Dhu Teh, and Deng Xiaoping.

November 1956–March 1957
Visits India to participate in twenty-five hundredth anniversary of Buddha's birth, called *Jayanti* celebration.

February 1959
Receives Geshe Lharampa degree, doctor of Buddhist studies, during *Monlam* ceremonies in Lhasa.

March 17, 1959
Escapes with family, government leaders, and followers from Norbulingka Palace in Lhasa. Begins dangerous trek into exile.

March 30, 1959
Crosses border into India after fourteen-day journey.

April 30, 1960
Arrives in Dharamsala, India, to take up permanent residence.

1962
My Land and My People published.

September–November 1973
First visit to the West (Italy, Switzerland, the Netherlands, Belgium, Ireland, Norway, Sweden, Denmark, United Kingdom, West Germany, and Austria).

December 10, 1989
Awarded Nobel Prize for Peace in Oslo, Norway.

1990
Freedom in Exile: The Autobiography of the Dalai Lama published.

1998
The Art of Happiness: A Handbook for Living published.

2001
The Heart of Compassion: A Practical Approach to a Meaningful Life published.

October 17, 2007
Awarded U.S. Congressional Gold Medal in Washington, D.C.

August 5, 2008
Sends greetings to Beijing, wishing Chinese government success with its upcoming Summer Olympic Games.

April 2009
Visits California and Massachusetts.

June 8, 2009
Tours France and receives honorary citizenship of Paris.

September–October 2009
Tours United States and Canada.

For Further Reading

Books

Laurie Dolphin, *Our Journey from Tibet*. New York: Penguin, 1997. The gripping story of three sisters who risk everything to escape Tibet and flee to exile. Features a photo-essay showing the Dalai Lama greeting new arrivals in Nepal.

Tenzin Gyatso, the Fourteenth Dalai Lama of Tibet, *Freedom in Exile: The Autobiography of the Dalai Lama*. New York: HarperCollins, 1990. The Dalai Lama's second autobiography tells his life story and much background about Tibet. Also contains photographs of the Dalai Lama's life, both in Tibet and in exile.

Claire Harrahan, editor, *Opposing Viewpoints: Tibet*. Greenhaven Press, Farmington Hills: 2009. Provides both sides of the Tibetan– Chinese issue.

Heinrich Harrer, *Seven Years in Tibet*. New York: Tarcher/Penguin, 2009. Originally published in 1953. The story of Harrer's escape from a prisoner of war camp in India, his perilous journey across Tibet, and his friendship with the Dalai Lama.

His Holiness the Dalai Lama and Howard C. Cutler, *The Art of Happiness: A Handbook for Living*. New York: Riverhead, 1998. Combining psychiatry and Buddhism, the Dalai Lama and Cutler explore how to cope with life's problems, pressures, and relationships through stories, conversations, and meditations.

His Holiness the Dalai Lama of Tibet, *My Land and My People*. New York: McGraw-Hill, 1962. The Dalai Lama's first autobiography, written soon after leaving Tibet.

His Holiness the Dalai Lama, *Becoming Enlightened*. New York: Simon & Schuster, 2009. Step-by-step exercises to expand the reader's capacity for spiritual growth, using personal anecdotes and an accessible practical approach. For people of all faiths.

Elizabeth Cody Kimmel, *Boy on the Lion Throne: The Childhood of the Dalai Lama*. New York: Roaring Brook, 2009. A children's biography of the Dalai Lama's early years, before his forced exile.

Patricia K. Kummer, *Tibet*. New York: Scholastic, 2003. Tibet's geography and history.

Steve Lehman, Mark Bailey, and Robert Barnett, *The Tibetans: A Struggle to Survive*. Brooklyn, NY: Umbrage Editions, 1999. Record of the ten-year tour and study of ravaged Tibet by author Steve Lehman. Formatted in scrapbooklike style, with striking photos of the people and places of "modern" Tibet.

Tom Morgan, ed., *A Simple Monk: Writings on His Holiness the Dalai Lama*. Novato, CA: New World Library, 2001. A collection of articles about the Dalai Lama by admirers, scholars, and followers of the Dalai Lama. Lavishly illustrated.

Whitney Stewart, *14th Dalai Lama: Spiritual Leader of Tibet*. New York: Lerner, 2000. The life of the Dalai Lama, the history of Tibet, and an introduction to Buddhism.

DVDs

Biography: Dalai Lama—The Soul of Tibet. A&E Home Video, 2005. The series' biography of the Dalai Lama, with personal interviews, behind-the-scenes footage, and commentary.

Dalai Lama Renaissance. Wakan Films, 2009. Narrated by Harrison Ford, this film documents the Dalai Lama's conference in Dharamsala at the end of the twentieth century, featuring open discussions with forty of the world's most innovative thinkers.

Kundun. Martin Scorsese, director. Touchstone Pictures/Walt Disney Video, 1998. The landmark movie about the life of the Dalai Lama, from birth to exile. Rated PG-13.

Little Buddha. Bernardo Bertolucci, director. Miramax, 1994. A movie about the fictional search and discovery of a reincarnated Tibetan Buddhist lama. Also features background story of the life and enlightenment of Siddhartha, the Indian prince who became the Buddha, with Keanu Reeves. Offers a look inside a Tibetan Buddhist monastery and its temple as well. Rated PG.

Seven Years in Tibet. Jean-Jacques Annaud, director. SONY Pictures, 2003. The film version of Heinrich Harrer's autobiography. Starring Brad Pitt. Rated PG-13.

Tibet: A Buddhist Trilogy. Festival Media, 2006. Highly acclaimed documentary, first released in 1979. Three parts discuss the Dalai Lama, monastic life, and the Buddhist concept of impermanence.

Unwinking Gaze: The Inside Story of the Dalai Lama's Struggle for

Tibet. IndiePix Films, 2009. A three-year behind-the-scenes look at the Dalai Lama's frustrating attempts to negotiate with China.

Web Sites

Dalai Lama Foundation (www.dalailamafoundation.org). A user-friendly site, also associated with the Foundation for Universal Responsibility but with drop-down menus for various departments, including one for youth that features a Peace Wall blog site and an ethics game. Also contains a link to Project Happiness Web site.

Foundation for Universal Responsibility of His Holiness the Dalai Lama (www.furhhdl.org). The Dalai Lama's foundation's official Web site, funded in part with money he was awarded as part of the Nobel Peace Prize in 1989. Contains links to speeches, conferences, and news articles dealing with the foundation.

The Government of Tibet in Exile (www.tibet.com). The official Web site of Tibet's government in exile in Dharamsala.

His Holiness the 14th Dalai Lama of Tibet (www.dalailama .com). The Dalai Lama's official Web site, featuring photos and links to articles about Tibet's history, the Dalai Lama's life, and his activities.

Nobelprize.org (www.nobelprize.org). The official Web site of the Nobel Prize Committee in Oslo, Norway. Contains information about each of the prizewinners, as well as activities for children that deal with and encourage peace.

Project Happiness (www.projecthappiness.com). Project Happiness was founded in 2006 by Randy Taran with the help and support of the Dalai Lama. Headquartered in Palo Alto, California, its Web site offers lots of activities and links for kids and teachers.

Picture Credits

Cover: © Doane Gregory/Sygma/Corbis
© Alison Wright/Corbis, 59
© Anindito Mukherjee/epa/Corbis, 81
© Bajonski/Alamy, 82
© Bettmann/Corbis, 15, 23, 30, 34–35, 42, 44–45, 48–49, 55, 62
© Galen Rowell/Corbis, 60
© Jayanta Shaw/Reuters/Corbis, 7
John Dominis/Time Life Pictures/Getty Images, 57
© Keren Su/Corbis, 19
Keystone/Hulton Archive/Getty Images, 38
© Manjunath Kiran/epa/Corbis, 70
Popperfoto/Getty Images, 18, 51
© Radek Pietruszka/epa/Corbis, 74–75
© Raymond Darolle/Sygma/Corbis, 68
© Reuters/Corbis, 65
© STR/Keystone/Corbis, 31
Tatyana Makeyeva/AFP/Getty Images, 11
Tim Zielenback/AFP/Getty Images, 76
© Trapper Frank/Corbis Sygma, 71
Vecchio/Three Lions/Getty Images, 28
William Bacon/Photo Researchers, Inc., 25

Charles George and Linda George have been writing children's nonfiction books for more than ten years. They have nearly sixty books in print on a wide variety of subjects—from ancient civilizations to world religions, from the Holocaust to civil rights and black nationalism, from working dogs to the world's pyramids. Charles and Linda were both teachers in Texas schools before "retiring" to write. They live in a small town in West Texas.